Forew

I would like to thank all the people who helped proof read this book and give me guidance and support.
I am eternally grateful to everyone who helped me on the journey that led to the path I now walk.
I would also like to apologise to all the people who I have hurt over the years who suffered because of my addictions.

NOT LIKE THIS - *By Derek Mills*

It's always difficult to start a story that hinges on so many different events and that are all on a very complicated time line. So I've decided to start at the end, which is also the beginning. Bear with me as I unravel a very messed up ball of string. This story is going to be like riding a rollercoaster through the hall of mirrors and sometimes I will remember things at the most unusual times and tell you all about them. My mind has been really messed up through drink and drug abuse and I think you'll get a real measure of that as we go on.

But, before I tell you my story I need you to know a couple of things..

Firstly it's that the Bible tells us 3 times a very clear message of hope. Firstly in the book of JOEL 2:32, then in ACTS 2:21 and finally in Romans 10:13.

The message is a cry into the darkness, a shout in the wilderness, it is a message for the broken and the lost, just like me and maybe, just like you!

It is, that

"ALL WHO CALL UPON THE LORD WILL BE SAVED"

The second point I need you to be aware of, is that this promise of salvation comes hand in hand with a remedy to the turmoil in our souls and it is that 'Jesus is a light in the darkness'.

The book of John 8:12 gives a very clear instruction, a promise, in the Bible it is known as a covenant, which is more than any promise we can make, it is an 'unbreakable' agreement with God. WOW,!
…it is that we can be saved and live in the light!

John 8:12

"I am the light of the world. Whoever follows me will never walk in darkness, but will have the light of life."

The Darkness

In 2008 I was a very different person. My life was chaotic to say the least. I was running two very successful businesses, with several people working for me. I owned a house on one of the most popular streets in town, I had a lovely young family with 2 beautiful sons. We went on several holidays every year and we bought whatever we wanted.

To everyone around me, my life must have looked perfect. I was living a life driven by self, greed and envy. I thought I was better than everyone else and that I deserved much more than you.

The bible tells us in…

Mark 8:36

'What good is it for someone to gain the whole world, yet forfeit their soul?'

Maybe this is you?

However, if you actually knew me back then, you would have either been drugged and drunk with me, living in the mad dream world I existed in, or you would be crossing the road to avoid me.
Looking back I would have hated having me as a neighbour. I had no respect for myself let alone anyone else.

The good morning madness

My life was complete insanity. A normal working day would start with feeling sick, very sick. I would be shaking and nauseous, trying to pretend that this was just how it was and that everything was normal. Super strong coffee to wash away the foul taste in my mouth and a big fat joint to stop the shaking was my daily morning routine.

Usually it was only half a joint, as somehow I'd usually managed to smoke the pre prepared 'medicine' the night before. This would calm my shaking just enough to roll the next. I would usually get some sort of sorry look and head shaking from my wife, or a barrage of questions, like. 'How did you get home last night?", "Where have you been?", 'where's the van?'.

There were days when I would swear blind I'd walked home, only to find my van stuffed into the hedge outside my house, door still open and empty beer bottles spilling out.

Then an argument would ensue about drink driving, how irresponsible I am etc etc Blah, Blah, Blah,… whatever, shut up, don't you know easy your life is? You don't need to work, I earn all the money in this house, who do you think you are to tell me how I should relax on an evening… don't you even know how hard I work?

Wasn't this just how we all started our day?, because this was normal in my world.

And this was all before 8am! However, now, with weed flowing through my brain, my hands were as calm as an assassins cross hairs, I'd put my wife in her place, justified my existence and I was ready to go out an make a shed load of cash.

I would jump into the van, off my head, pick up the lads and head off to whatever job the day held. I spent my days landscaping gardens, concreting down at the dockyards or putting up prison fencing!

Life was rosey and all was well, until that itch started in my head, the little voices suggesting a quick lunchtime pint; the lads will love you for that; you're a great boss after all. So executive decision made, down tools and off to the pub we go… only that pint very quickly turns into five and that familiar pleasant buzz, that calmness, soon relieves my anxiety and soothes the nerves. I was now invincible, full of promises and so, Now back to work.

You see, on the inside, my head was a mess, always looking over my shoulder to see if I'd been caught out, hoping that my amazing ability to drive home completely mashed would not bring my attention to the Police. Hoping that I wold get through another day without my wife finding out about whatever it happened to be that I'd been up to.

I was living a life of abject horror, deep misery and a paranoia beyond belief.

Looking back now, it is clear that I was chronically depressed, living a daily life deep within a full mental breakdown and completely unaware of my undiagnosed mental health issues. My days continuously revolved around the acquisition of money, alcohol and drugs. I could barely go a couple of hours without my medicine or sorting out how to get more. I was always afraid that today would be the day I'd get found out.

I was living life in a dark world filled with lying, cheating, drunkenness, stealing and I hated every moment of my life. I was starting to get noticed and processed by the Police, which led to cautions for fighting and drug possession, but that's another story!

Maybe this is you?

Business or pleasure

I once tried my hand at cocaine dealing. so a friend and I drove over to Manchester to purchase a couple of ounces of uncut cocaine. This was one of the most terrifying nights of my life. I was about to enter what felt like the script of a horror movie.

We met a scrawny little, bedraggled man in the corner of some dodgy pub, somewhere on the outskirts of Manchester. This is what we had been instructed to do. I cant remember the name or location of the pub, but believe me when I say, it is not a place any normal person would go to enjoy a quiet pint!

We had a very short conversation regarding what was going to be the next step. Firstly we were to hand over several thousand pounds to someone we didn't know. This is the point where you imagine the newspaper report and conversations saying' who in their right mind would do that?' And, 'what did they expect?' .

Of course, I think you are starting to realise that I was certainly not in my right mind. Then the weasley little man, with very few words, and certainly nothing that would be considered a conversation, instructed us to follow him.

The route took us down and around some dodgy streets, to a scruffy looking doorway to a house, on some scary, run down terrace. On arrival the scrawny man sculked off and we followed our last instruction. We had were to knock, enter the door and wait.

By this time our nerves were jangling and I was wondering if any of this was worth it. We all make stupid decisions in life and I was starting to think this was probably going to top them all. But it was to get much worse. We entered the door of the end terrace, back to back house, typical of the poorer areas of many big cities. The door opened, we noticed our arrival had been monitored by the many cctv cameras pointing up and down the road. Opening the door we were greeted by stairs straight ahead of us and a reinforced steel door to the right.

Terrifyingly, at the top of the stairs, was a bloke sat behind some sort of giant old WW2 machine gun, pointed right down at us! Man alive, I felt like I was going to pass out. I thought that this was it, the last stupid decision of my life. I was about to become a statistic in some grimy news story. However, with nothing else left to do and our pockets very empty, we followed our next instruction and gingerly knocked on the steel door. There was a brief pause before the little hatch slid open and a hand holding our small package emerged.

Buying drugs like this is nothing like it is in the movies. You don't get to check the merchandise, poke your knife into it and rub your gums. No, you give the man your money, get what your given and leave. No warranty, no guarantees, no weighing, nothing. Just stay calm, take your gear and walk away.

We took the product, if you've never seen an ounce of cocaine, its not what you expect. Imagine half a fun size mars bar and thats it. The movies image of bags full of cocaine would cost tens or hundreds of thousands of pounds. We were mere tadpoles in the ocean. We hurried away, back through the maze of streets to the car. We couldn't get away quick enough. Images of us being done over and getting robbed fills our paranoid minds. The doors locked, the engine roared to life and we shot off, back towards the M62 and home. Our wives awaited our call and as soon as we could we phoned them to say mission successful. Mind at this point we hadn't even loomed at our parcel! For all we knew it could have been a fun size mars bar!

Driving back home that night was so stressful. We had enough cocaine on us to secure a lengthy stay at her majesty's pleasure and to say we were paranoid that night, is a huge understatement. Our nerves were on edge as we drove our precious cargo home. Were we driving at the right speed? Not too fast? not too slow?

Did we look like normal relaxed adults just driving a normal journey on the motorway? The more you try to look normal, the less normal you look!

We soon decided to pull up at the next service station to calm our nerves, we still had about an hours drive before we would be safely home and dry. This was the moment of truth. Had we been scammed? Or did we have two ounces of the 'top quality uncut gear' we had been promised by our source. My fingers fumbled as I unwrapped the solid cling filmed lump that had been stuffed in my mates pocket. A cd case was produced and there it was, the biggest lump of cocaine I'd ever seen for real. We very quickly and discreetly scrape a couple of lines out onto the cd case and within seconds we knew that this was good gear!

Man alive, we'd both never had such good quality cocaine. Our heads were on fire and the ecstatic buzz shot through our whole bodies. My mind was going into overdrive. I knew that when I got home I could cut this up with caffeine tablets, and I could double my money. The terror of acquiring the gear had passed, it was all just par for the course. Soon I would be making the money!

Well that was the plan.

We arrived back home and cut the lump into two pieces. Now was not the night to socialise, tonight was business. All I had to do was go home and get cutting. However, that's not how it went. You see theres a saying…' and open bag is an empty bag' and three days later, with no sleep and a constantly bleeding nose, it was clear that cocaine dealing was not my forte. I thought I'd have just having one more little line, but soon I had managed to snort the whole lot.

This little venture had cost me £1300 and three nights sleep.

It had become very clear, that I was also a really rubbish cocaine dealer!

So getting back to my life…

Despite the fact that to everyone around me, my life looked great, I was constantly driven by an insane and insatiable need to find oblivion… every day.

Maybe this is you?

I hated everything and everyone. I was angry all the time, but mostly I hated being me. Being in my head was the absolute definition of hell. The voices drove me to do stupid things, to make irrational choices and to do it all at the expense of the people I loved most. Most people think hell is a place you only go if you die. I can assure you hell can be lived in right here and now. Its where I spent m most of my time.

The Bible tells it so…

Jude 6 - *Hell is a prison of everlasting chains from which there is no hope of release*

Matthew 13 - *it is a furnace of conscious torment, where the fire never goes out*

Mark 9 - *it is a place of excruciating misery where the worm does not die*

These verses describe exactly what life in my head was like.

Everyday, as much as I promised myself each night (and I was constantly trying to make a real, full hearted decision that somehow I was going to crack the issue myself), and before passing out, I would beg the God I didn't believe in, that tomorrow would be different, but as usual I always messed everything up.

The real sad part of al this was the look on my wife's face most mornings. It was heartbreaking. The sorry looking shake of her head and that sad pitiful expression, said it all.

There were constant broken promises to my two, beautiful little boys, there were hundreds, if not thousands of, 'it will be different next times'. The only thing to shut the noise ion my head up was those first few drinks. Everyday just added another self hating thought to the last, it was like a millstone of disappointing misery hanging, no dragging, my face along the path of ruined good intentions!

Maybe this is you?

Time for Action

So I decided it was time for action, it was time to bring this misery to an end. I was a grown man and it was time to sort this sorry mess out myself. I had over the years at many times tried to make the ultimate and final decision. On a few occasions I would stand at the hard shoulder of the motorway looking at the lorries thundering along, thinking, 'just one more step'. Then a ridiculous irrational voice in my head would suggest stupid tings to me like, 'what about the poor lorry driver'. I would get so cross at myself, as the moment would pass and 'one more step' was not going to happen today. Maybe next time.

Without glamourising my suicidal thoughts, its as I write this I am called to think of the irrationality of the whole concept of the internal argument that gets in the way of the 'final step'. I remember visiting my sister and her partner with my wife and kids. He was an active member of the PSNI in Northern Ireland and as such he was always armed with a Glock 9mm pistol. We were staying in their lovely new house and we're being given 'the tour'. It was whilst I was in their lovely new kitchen that he produced his gun to show me. Very much a man thing. He warned me that it was always loaded, so do not pull the trigger. The feeling of that gun in my had awoke something inside me. I remember the look on his face as I lifted the gun and put it to my head.

This was it, the moment I'd been waiting for… just one little squeeze and it would all be over. 'Derek'. He said very calmly, 'please give me the gun'. I however was in a different world.

When it happened it was like there was a bubble around me, it an other world feeling and everything around me was muffled. There was just that little voice saying ' just one little squeeze'!

And then, as usual, that other totally irrational voice saying 'but just think of the mess in their new kitchen'! And that's it. The moment is lost with that overriding voice. The voice of God?

The only thing that stopped me from pulling the trigger, (a rare opportunity for a suicidal depressive) was the thought of the mess it would make. Like that would have been everyone's main worry if I had just done it. But I was a failure and couldn't even get this right.

By this point in time, I had been thrown out of the house. Having a drunken drug addict around is not a nice experience for anyone. I also had all means of finance taken away from me, bank cards etc. You see, I'd spent every bit of money available to the family, all my accounts were less than empty, the boys piggy banks were raided, my wife's wages at her weekend shifts at the pub went straight into paying my tab and more. I was an absolute liability both financially and physically. A danger to myself and others.

On a really sad note, I was actually proud of the fact that not only was I the only person in the pub to have a tab, but I also was the only person to have there own entry line on the pub account spreadsheets!

Minor victories should be taken at any opportunity.

What kind of sad and twisted idiot chalks that one up as one of life's great achievements.

I was also at this time, living in a dirty, old £400 caravan. Not that it was quite that bad when we bought it. After I left, my wife had trouble even giving it away. I think the bloke who took it housed his dogs in it. I lived there so that my children wouldn't see me in the terrible states I got myself in. My life had gotten so low, I was now also doing whatever it took to find money.

Im not proud of any of the things I did, but addiction will eventually drag the very best of people into the darkest of places.

My wife was allocating me £10 per day for fags and booze etc, which was no where near enough to pay for the amount of drink or drugs I needed. I was writhing my painful way through each day, and by this time I was also no longer able to work. I'd lost my lucrative prison contract after being complained about and being found drunk and stoned in a prison! It was not just me losing my job, but the teams of lads working for became unemployed too.

These last moths, weeks and days were a nightmare within a nightmare! I was living in the actual pit of hell and satan was my mentor.

Maybe this is you?

My time in Prison

Despite being a raging addict, I was actually very good at what I did work wise. I could talk my way into just about any job contract, selling the abilities of myself and my team to accomplish whatever the jobs required. If I didn't know what to do I'd look it ups on the internet, change my company website and just blatantly lie. From installing a small fence at a school in Yorkshire, I had then managed to wangle a lucrative contract installing prison fencing.

It was whilst working an a category A prison, that I nearly ended up as an inmate. I had somehow managed to blag an amazing contract working in prisons all over the UK erecting fencing. The great thing was that I got paid for every man I took through the gates with me. I had several men working in different locations around the country all making me money. I felt like a god.

The scary fact about it, was that most of the lads I employed should have probably been inmates themselves, had been or have probably become so since.

If you've ever entered a prison you'll know how long it can take and the bureaucracy involved.. Each day involves going vehicle by vehicle through the 'air lock'. This is where the security guards isolated you and the vehicle, do their random searches.

They check in your van, open a few tool boxes and frisk everyone on your team. They then log you in and this certifies you for the day. Then the big door opens and in you go to work.

As a prison contractor, your every move is monitored. You are accompanied everywhere, through every gate or door and every movement is logged. Hardly any work gets done each day because of this bureaucracy and jobs that would normally take weeks, last for months. This is the best bit, as a job which would normally take a week or two, actually takes months. And you get paid for the whole time you're there.

The contract also included expenses, hotels, food and very importantly my beer. The pub next to where we stayed had to run an extra beer pump at the bar solely for us and the amount we all drank. The locals were not too happy and we made a menace of ourselves, but the landlord loved us!

It was one day in prison, whilst getting some tools from the van, that I noticed the big bag of weed in the glove box, along with my eight inch divers knife, mobile phone and two shotgun shells. This was right in the middle of a category A prison. Only an addict can really understand the drug induced paranoia that this situation brought about. Lets face it, no normal person would ever get into such a pickle. Just taking a phone into prison is a chargeable offence.

At the days end, and after safely making our way out of the prison, I thoroughly searched and emptied the van, we checked every nook and cranny in that van. I rebuked all my workers for not being vigilant enough and drilled them on the importance of caution. Like any of this was their fault.

It was a good job we stripped the van clean that evening as the very next day, whilst going through the air lock, the only place the security guards searched was the glove box! It was almost as if they had been told where to look.

God was with me back then and I didn't even know it. God had plans and me being in prison was certainly not one of them. I shudder now as I think about the potentially negative, life altering situations I was getting myself and indeed, my friends into. I was walking a very fine line and the stakes were high.

The final solution

So, solution time. The magical plan I had been formulating was upon me. I had been working up to this moment for many years and it wasn't taken lightly.

I made a concerted effort to stay a sober as possible so that I could come into the house to say goodnight to my children. I hugged then tightly and reassured them that Daddy loved them so much. Then I phoned all my friends and family for a chat. I didn't want anyone accidentally calling me or popping by for a visit that evening. Too be honest, I have no recollection of what I said to them.

I then locked the caravan door and lined up all the drink and drugs I'd managed to get hold of. Then I turned on the broken gas fire with its big thick yellow flame and said goodbye to the world that hated me. I said goodbye to the me who hated me! I quickly drank gin by the bottle mixed with strong lager and frosty jack cider, took magic mushrooms and smoked some fat joints.

Finally, after years of torment I was going to be free. The devil must have been singing for his supper and I was on the menu. The carbon monoxide combined with the drink and drugs, were about to slowly caress me into an eternal sleep. I don't recall passing out, it was that easy.

Goodbye cruel world I'm leaving you today…(I love a bit of Pink Floyd)

BUT…

God had other plans

At some point the following day I started to come too. It was the most peculiar sensation. There was a sound I could hear like a phone ringing quietly at the end of a 40 foot drainpipe. Over and over and over. Man alive, my head was thick, it felt like being stuck in porridge. I felt very very dizzy and I felt very, very strange.

Again, there was that noise, over and over again.

Very slowly I started to come around, I was really panicking now as I couldn't move properly, I tried to stand up, but I couldn't walk. My limbs felt like lead.
I crawled to the door. And boy it was hot in the van. And I couldn't breath very well… and there was still that ringing noise? That constant ringing.

I don't know when or how it happened but at some point I'd gone to the effort of stripping copper wire and binding the door handle shut from the inside.

I now realise this was to prevent anyone getting in to stop me, or specifically so my boys would not find their dad dead.

Frantically I unravelled the wire, my fingers tearing at the twisted metal, but eventually I fell out of the caravan door and onto the gravel drive. I was half alive, half dead, and my head was pounding. Damn and double damn, what had gone wrong? Why was I still alive? I was so cross with myself. This had been my grand finalé. Working up to these moments takes a lot of mental planning and cant be taken lightly. The courage required to pull the trigger, jump or whatever is beyond measure. So I was no happy I'd failed.

I'd only gone and overlooked the vent holes in the caravan floor! I'd taken every other measure during my preparation, just to overlook some little holes. Had I seen them I would have blocked them all up. Every caravan has them, especially to stop people from 'accidentally' gassing themselves.
There must have been just enough air getting in to the van to keep me alive, how had I forgotten this?

Crumpled up on the gravel, I tried to stand up. It was then that a voice, resounding like a giant bell, resonated right through me saying..

"*NOT LIKE THIS*".

But the voice wasn't mine!

I had cried out to a God I didn't believe in to

'HELP ME'.

I've spoken with many atheists over the years and I can assure you, even those who proclaim that God is not real, always find themselves praying the unbelievers prayer…

'God, if you get me out of this situation, I'll believe in you!'

These are the prayers of the drunk driver, or the person caught sleeping around, the person who's lie is about to be found out..etc.

These are the situations in life, where suddenly, you are now miraculously open to the idea that there might actually be a god! And, you even go as far as to entertain a prayer!

Temptation

In the Bible in Matthew 4, the Devil tries to get Jesus to prove he is God. Satan demands he does miracles to demonstrate his power but, unfortunately my friend, it is up to us to prove ourselves to him and not the other way around. God is real, of that I'm 100% certain.

Matthew 4 - Jesus Is Tested in the Wilderness

1 Then Jesus was led by the Spirit into the wilderness to be tempted by the devil.

2 After fasting forty days and forty nights, he was hungry.

3 The tempter came to him and said, "If you are the Son of God, tell these stones to become bread."

4 Jesus answered, "It is written: 'Man shall not live on bread alone, but on every word that comes from the mouth of God.'"

5 Then the devil took him to the holy city and had him stand on the highest point of the temple.

6 *"If you are the Son of God," he said, "throw yourself down. For it is written:*

*"'He will command his angels concerning you,
   and they will lift you up in their hands,
   so that you will not strike your foot against a stone.'"*

7 *Jesus answered him, "It is also written: 'Do not put the Lord your God to the test.'"*

8 *Again, the devil took him to a very high mountain and showed him all the kingdoms of the world and their splendour.*

9 *"All this I will give you," he said, "if you will bow down and worship me."*

10 *Jesus said to him, "Away from me, Satan! For it is written: 'Worship the Lord your God, and serve him only.'"*

11 *Then the devil left him, and angels came and attended him.*

Has this ever been you?

So, filled with fear and dread, with my frazzled brain desperately trying to make sense of the dire situation I was in, and feeling more depressed than ever, I made my way to the doctors. A voice within me started to ask, did I really want to die? Like that? Did I really want my children to remember their Dad like that, a sorry, dead, drunken drug addict, lying in his own filth in an old caravan?

The devil was laughing at me now, he was filling my thoughts with a barrage of self hatred. The screeching joy of Satan was overwhelming in my head, saying things like, 'Your a disgrace!, a coward!, and you cant even kill yourself properly! I really was an absolute loser! But God had other plans.

…And the phone that kept ringing! That was my little baby brother. He was desperately trying to call me, over and over he called and I seem to remember there were at least 19 missed calls from him.

To this day he won't tell me about the conversation I had with him the night before, but his persistence woke me up just enough that I didn't die.

God uses people around us all the time, even if they are not believers. It is clear now that God commissioned my little brother to do his earthly work and I will never forget this. I am certain that his calls saved my life.

This was Monday 8th September 2008 at approx 11am.

Rehab costs how much?

I cant remember how I got there, but the doctor poked and prodded me, shook his head and told me that I probably had 2 - 3 weeks to live. He commented that I was a completely hopeless case and that he held out little hope for my future.

He suggested I try Rehab. He looked on his computer, tapped a few keys and then told me that the news was not good. NHS rehab had a 9 month waiting list, as I'd rejected earlier interventions, or not turned up for 'therapy' blah, blah, blah, he flippantly said I would not survive next month, never mind nine months. His only hope for me was a private rehab and as I departed his office he gave me a telephone number.

At this point I was also already heavily addicted to librium. I'd lied to the doctors about trying to stop drinking over the past many months and they kept giving me these 'home detox' drugs. I loved them and they were free.

My mind was numb and I made my way slowly home, feeling worse than ever. How had my life come to this! Only ten years earlier I was a proud sailor in the Royal Navy, sharp, witty and full of positive life, full of promise and expectations. What the hell had gone wrong?

At home I slumped at the computer, looked up the rehab centre and instantly died inside. My life was suddenly filled with further despair, as the 6 week 12 step detox & recovery came with an £8500 price tag! Where was the justice in this world? I now knew for certain that I had no chance, I was in so much debt, that my only glimmer of hope was gone. Not just that, I was so useless, I couldn't even kill myself properly

Because God still had other plans!

Unbeknownst to me, my wife had been frantically phoning my Mam. Everyone was always talking about me behind my back and any addict will know the paranoia that comes with these phone calls and discussions.

Everyone is always tying to fix us, formulating plans for our issues, moaning about our weak will, the - '*doesn't he know he has a beautiful family*', '*surely he should show a bit of will power*', '*why would anyone behave that way*;, etc etc etc.

However, this time was different. My lovely beautiful Mam, the most loving mam you'll ever meet, the mam who put up with so much heartache, directly caused by me and my addiction. My mam, who had been desperately waiting for years and years, in fact, a lifetime, to hear me ask for help, she, with an abundance of love and importantly, hope, booked me into that private rehab centre!

I have a mother and father who never gave up on me.

Luke 15:31-32

"'My son,' the father said, 'you are always with me, and everything I have is yours. But we had to celebrate and be glad, because this brother of yours was dead and is alive again; he was lost and is found.'"

I'm a gonna go to rehab baby, yeah, yeah, yeah

On Wednesday 10 September 2008, knowing that my life would soon change, I organised a 'going to rehab party'. As I write this, I think of the insanity of the idea of a going away party. Maybe I'd watched too many movies, but at the time it really did seem like the right thing to do, and I was very, very excited.

The usual suspects attended. Me and my fellow alcoholics and drug addicts got together to have one last blow out, one more ride around the block and this was going to be the party of the year. All on a random Wednesday in September. It never mattered what the day was, every day could be celebrated by an addict.

An addict will take any opportunity to maximise the moment and this was as good as any. In fact, this was an awesome reason to really go for it. Birthdays are a great excuse for a party and so are wakes. A sunny day gets the BBQ going and that becomes a party. A rainy day and we'll commiserate the lack of sun and it becomes a good reason to have house party. A new job, losing a job, a great day at work or a crap one. A day that ends in a Y. Whatever the reason is, an addict will engineer the perfect reason for a crazy session and this day was no different. The fact that I had no money was also important, as everyone would be buying me my drinks tonight. Cheers guys, heres one for the road.

I always messed things up

Looking back again, I wonder how I even made it to the Rehab unit. Insanity was truly my middle name and I'm not even sure if that's a hard enough word to describe it. But the 'blowout' went ahead regardless. My crazy drink and drug addicted friends, like me, all thought this a great idea, wasn't it 'wacky Wednesday' after all! (Most days had a name, as if adding humour to a self destructive addiction somehow made everything ok). I can only assume my devastated wife was desperately calling my parents to try to stop something terrible from happening.

My drinking had begun to come hand in hand with 'incidents'. I would come around some mornings covered in blood, or with huge bruises on my body. One morning I woke up with my face stuck to a bloodied pillow and hurting. I made my way to the bathroom to examine the pain, only to find hundreds of black thorns embedded in my face. I'd obviously fallen into the hedge on my way home. I am amazed I didn't blind myself.

Anyway, I digress. At this time, while I was literally partying my life away, my parents were already in the car and desperately driving their way down from Berwick-upon-Tweed to the sleepy market town of Brigg. And all the while I was rapidly descending into a drunk to end them all.

The madness of my life would see me phone the pub whilst on the way there, to get the barman to prepare two pints on the bar, ready for my arrival and as I quaffed them in just a couple of seconds, the third would be poured. Then I could relax and enjoy the fourth pint. On an average lunchtime I would, drink about five pints of strong lager, whether I was working or not and driving was just a technicality.

Often on my way back home, after a hard days work I would head straight to my local. Now this is where a deep sadness fuelled my depression. I usually had to drive past my house. I would be driving in my very obvious, sign written work van. I would be praying that the children weren't back from school. If I drove past an empty house I was happy to justify going for a 'couple' after work. If I saw my wife's car in the drive, I felt a pain in my heart deeper than anyone can imagine as this meant my children were home from school. The paranoia that they may see daddy's van drive past the window, could only be washed away by a pint.

Except an afternoon pint was usually about twelve pint of Stella, and a sesh would see me drink up to twenty four! Well, I did deserve them, after all I did work very, very hard.

Like many nights before, the drinks flowed, glasses were raised, the pub was filled with demonic laughter, as each of my 'friends' systematically poisoned me and boy did I lap it up. I was the centre of all the attention, drinking it down and wondering after all, if I really needed rehab.
I mean, we were having fun yes? Whats wrong with a bit of fun?

Maybe this is like your life?.. Or maybe, not yet?

I'm not quite sure what we all thought the outcome of a session in rehab was going to be, but it would probably stop everyone from moaning on at me. Yes, I would show them all! They would all see, all along, just how wrong they were and that I would return refreshed and ready to start drinking normally, like a gentleman. However, there was never anything normal about my drinking, I always had one or five too many and nearly always messed things up. Nearly always?? No, retract that, *I always messed things up!*

How that night ended, to this day I will never know, though it usually ended up with me being left in the beer garden, with a few pints lined up on the table and the pub locked up behind me.

The next two days are a blur as my drinking had, over the past year, been taken to a whole new level. I have fleeting memories of my dad sitting in the caravan with me as I smoked weed and mushrooms, and drank gin by the pint. He sat there pouring my booze away as quick as I could drink it, making sure I didn't pass out and choke on my vomit, until eventually Friday morning was here and miraculously I was still alive. Now about the gin.! How did a man with no money drink gin by the bottle?

The lorry crash that nearly killed me

You may be wondering where all the gin came from that my dad was pouring away. Well only a few weeks before, I had received a phone call from my father in law to say that a lorry had crashed on the corner of the village.. and that there were bottles of gin and 12 year old whiskey all over the road and in the hedge. I was down there in my van like a rat up a drainpipe. It was like the movie 'whiskey galore'. It was like heaven to me and I dived into the pile of broken glass and alcohol with my welding gloves on. Within minutes the back of my van was brimming with the elixir of drunken life. I was buzzing, I had no money and the gods had answered all my prayers (except it was not God was it, this was clearly the work of Satan).

By lunchtime I'd sold all the whiskey. I was still a fussy drunk and I can't stand the smell of the stuff, Gin however is a deferent kettle of fish. With a splash of cordial, I could drink it by the pint! And it would hit the spot like a sledgehammer to the back of the head.

This abundance of booze took the final days to a new level and to be honest, the gin alone nearly killed me. So bottle by bottle my dad poured hundreds of pounds worth of gin down the sink.

D(tox)-Day

The next morning, I awoke, still alive but very sick, and my dad bathed me like a baby, shaved and dressed me in clean clothes and with great trepidation, we departed. I was sat in the back of my parents car. They strapped me in, we said goodbye and we set off on the death march to the nut house, a secure mental psychiatric detox unit in Barnsley.

I don't know who was scared the most on that journey, but I really do think it was my Mam and Dad. They were terrified that I was going to refuse to go at the very last minute and as every mile and every second went by, their anxiety grew, along with their hopes. But for me, I was content, I knew this was it and that I never had to live that life again. I knew the madness was over. I was completely broken and lived at the bottom of the deepest pit possible. I had ruined everything that was good in my life and I was so deep in the pit of hell that the darkness enveloped every cell of my body. It was on this day that I saw the very first spark of light.

I didn't know it then but that spark was the light of Jesus shining down at me.

John 8:12

I Am the Light of the World

Jesus spoke to them, saying, "I am the light of the world. Whoever follows me will not walk in darkness, but will have the light of life."

I can barely remember the first three days. I was very heavily medicated, nurses checked me half hourly and I was fed routinely. All this time I was coming down, from a wide range of street drugs, alcohol and a plethora of prescription medications.

For months I'd been taking librium like smarties and the detox unit had to give me massive doses to get me through. If you've ever seen the film 'Trainspotting' you'll have a pretty good idea of what a come down/ detox look like, only in here it was much, much cleaner. It was a dirty, filthy mess in my head though.

Day 1 of my new life

Friday 12 September 2008 was the first day of my new life. I had been deposited into the recovery unit and after 3 days of a heavily medicated detox, I began to come to my senses. For the first time in a very long while, I realised that it was all over. It was finished, I never needed to live that miserable drunken, drugged up life again.

It is only as I write this, that I see the significance in this rebirth.

To say I couldn't go a couple of hours without a drink or drug is an understatement and now, incredibly I had no desire to take anything. My desire and compulsion to drink or drug had gone! I cant emphasise this amazing transformation enough. Even a regular 'normal' person if asked not to drink ever again would become very anxious. But for me, that anxiety was n o longer.

Before, whenever I tried to quit, it was always a terrifying, painful battle that I knew I would lose. But this day was different, this was a true miracle. If you are suffering from addiction, you will certainly appreciate my amazed wonder of this release from the control substances have in your life.

If you'd seen me in that detox unit, writhing and crying, curled up sweating and shaking, running out of my room because of the black 'things' crawling on the walls and ceiling, the spiders under my skin, itching so bad; I'm sure if you'd seen that, you would have actually seen demons flying out of me, roaring like the sound of nails on a blackboard, an image like a scene from 'Raiders of the lost ark'. Demons are very, very real.

Jesus expelled demons from people during his time on earth and they are as real today as they were then. You probably find yourself sometimes saying, or hearing someone say 'he's got the devil in him'. Well, the devil rules this world we're in, and demons are running amok in the people around us. The devil is in the details of this broken world, worming his wickedness into everything you do. The look you give someone full of lust, the nasty thought in your head, these are the devil. The lust for fame and fortune, the sick desire to have what isn't yours. Jealousy and greed, the need to 'look' like you're better than everyone else even though it comes at a high personal cost. Hire purchase agreements, loans and credit cards, all designed to trap you in an unrealistic world, where your daily hard work will only ever cover the miserably high cost of paying off the interest.

Top tip: only pay for what you can afford. Saving for what you want in this world takes far less time than paying it off, and the reward is much more satisfying.

1 Peter 5:8

Be sober-minded; be watchful. Your adversary the devil prowls around like a roaring lion, seeking someone to devour.

…. however, the Devil is NOT a lion, he is a deceiver, a liar and he wants you to be afraid! He prowls 'like' a lion. The devil is a coward and he openly laughs at your weak desires for trinkets and shiny things, yet we still fall for his lure. Like a fish caught on a triple barbed hook, you will struggle at the expense of your life to shake yourself free. And many never do.

Recently, I heard a pastor give a talk on the Ten commandments. Most non believers and believer alike will state that these laws are archaic and not relevant. Why would a loving God demanded that..

"THOU SHALL NOT!" Do certain things.

This is a very misunderstood part of the Bible. God is making a covenant promise with us, that if we love him alone and have no other gods before him, then we …

'WILL' not' break his commands. The emphasis is on the word 'will'. It is a covenant promise of the freedom that comes through accepting God. This agreement 'frees us' from doing these things. With God, we 'will no longer' have to think about NOT following these amazing rules for a perfect existence, but rather, it it is something that just 'will not' happen. We will naturally live a life free of the misery that comes from breaking the rules.

* For example, if you do not pay for a parking ticket, 'thou shalt' get a fine!. If you always pay for a ticket, you 'will never' get a fine. It is an agreement.

So, in the detox unit, we were locked in a kind of prison block, (it was a secure mental facility really) only we had comfortable beds and nice food and I remember the nurses in the unit were lovely, I can't remember their names, but I will always remember their caring souls and calming manner.

I was surrounded by cleanliness, comfort and kindness. Its probably a strange thing to say, but I enjoyed the detox unit. For the first time in a very long time, I felt safe, primarily from myself, but also from the people who at the drop of a hat would help me get wasted again and I knew that the tornado of madness, insanity and misery that was my life, was over!

And, for the first time for as long as I could remember, I didn't want any drink or drugs. I didn't long for them, pine for them, in fact, I didn't even think about them.

Previously, with all the power I could muster, I had never been able to stop my self destructive behaviour. No matter what promises I made and to whoever I made them to, nothing worked.

I made and broke every promise you could possibly conjure up. I was able to make the most amazing promises to my wife and children, swearing on the name of the God I didn't believe in, that I would uphold my word on this occasion, but every time, and I mean absolutely every time, the promises I made were broken. I inflicted pain and anguish on everyone I loved and they despaired at my inability to do what I said.

But, it became clear over the next few weeks and months that GOD had been able to do something that I couldn't.

Luke 1:37

'Never let an impossible situation intimidate you. Why?

Because nothing is impossible with God'.

It is amazing as I look back on my life to see exactly where God was directing my life. Even in my darkest moments (and there were many), God had my hand. If you've ever read the poem 'footsteps', you will get a good idea of what I mean.

"Lord, you said once I decided to follow you, You'd walk with me all the way. But I noticed that during the saddest and most troublesome times of my life, there was only one set of footprints in the sand. I don't understand why, when I needed You the most, You would leave me." The Lord replied, "The times when you have seen only one set of footprints in the sand, is when I carried you". Amen

We were slowly introduced to Alcoholics Anonymous and at my very first AA meeting a man came to give us a talk about his recovery. I couldn't believe it, I was amazed, he had been clean and sober for six months! Man alive, I think I'd managed six hours, once, maybe, but this man looked healthy, stood straight and spoke clearly. There was hope in that room in abundance and I soaked it up with every pore in my body. One day, I would be that man.

The miracle of Gods healing touch stood right there in front of me and he was happy! No gritted teeth, no shaking and no lying. I don't know who you are, but you brought hope and light into a very dark time in my life.

Soon the detox week was over, I was clean inside and out, fed, watered and ready to move on. So one morning after breakfast, I said goodbye to the other inmates, hugged the nurses fondly and then a driver took me on the journey across the country to the sleepy little village of Thornton-le-dale in Yorkshire, to the recovery centre.

The first missing piece of jigsaw

The van pulled in to what looked a bit like a sprawling care home (in fact it had previously been an old folks home) and I was greeted by a member of staff. It felt like the day I'd arrived at Plymouth when I was 17 and joining the Royal Navy. I could see other people milling around trying to see the 'new recruit', these were the other 'inmates', and that's when I first saw the beautiful woman who would later become my wife.

What I didn't realise back then, but I soon became very clear on, was that just because I was clean and sober it didn't mean I wasn't still a complete and utter, raving lunatic! My mind was racing with new sensations and dreams of what could be, mixed with a big box of frogs. It would take a very long time and many hours in therapy to come even remotely close to normal, and I still don't think I'm quite there yet either, and as I write this its been 16 years since a drink or drug has passed my lips.

There was a lovely lady who was taking a lot of interest in me and I loved it. She was kind, generous, funny and so very beautiful. I would find gifts on my bed and I fancied the pants off her. The fact that I was a married man, as usual, meant absolutely nothing. I had never in my life fallen so instantly in love with anyone and being round her made me feel complete.

In fact, she felt like the 'missing piece of jigsaw' in my life and I was not going to let this moment go. She had been put there by God, for me and I was soon to find out she felt exactly the same way about me.

Before I'd had chance to say hello, I was taken to be processed. I filled in some forms and then I was searched for various contraband, including aftershave as its mostly 80% alcohol.

Man overboard!

When I served in the Royal Navy, I was onboard ship with a lad who I now know to have been a chronic alcoholic. Every day for him started with a few cans from the mess fridge, and he always drank the strong cider. Whilst at sea for a bit longer than usual, we ran out of booze and it was this was the first time I'd ever seen anyone drank a bottle of aftershave. It was one of those green bottles of Brut like my dad had and he, obviously, in sheer alcoholic desperation, supped the lot. - he later said he had the worst hangover he'd ever had, but that his sick smelled great!

It was at 3am one freezing cold night, whilst berthed in Plymouth sound, with snow on the decks, that this leading hand went to check up on the ratings working on a gantry off the rear end of our ship.

Being experienced and slightly sloshed, he decided he didn't need a safety harness. He leaned over to see how they were doing… and fell in. The 'man overboard' alarm sounded and the whole ship got up to see just what was going on. In true alcoholic style, a like of which I wouldn't experience until my journey took me down that path many years later, he was recovered from the sub zero sea clutching his can of cider with his freezing hands.

He had miraculously saved his precious booze, but lost his £150 prescription glasses. At the time we all laughed, he was taken to defrost in the Captains bath and life went on. The inherent sadness of this image, along with its tragically dark humour, is what chronic alcoholism looks like.

I hope and pray that he eventually found freedom from his addiction, but I've since learned that its probably less that 1% of 1% of addicts that ever get sobriety. Most suffer madness or an early death, and all will bring misery to their families and friends.

All of our prescription medication had to be handed over too. This was then dispensed daily, in a routine with the on site nurse, like something from a film. In fact one of the most played dvd's in the rehab centre was 'one flew over the cuckoo's nest'. A classic that resonated with all of us, and we all laughed overtime at the pure irony. I had truly 'gone fishing'.

After a week or so and If we followed the program, we were allowed to walk into the village, but only in threes. My future wife and I would take these opportunities to get close, to hold hands and steal kisses. Fraternisation in the rehab centre and in most recovery groups in general is a big no no.

Breaking the rules could get you expelled form the unit, but breaking rules was my speciality, I was good at it and it came naturally to me. So Jane and I thrived in our little 'outwith the world' bubble, where nothing was real. I don't know if it was wrong, but I was enjoying this peculiar, other worldly life where all I had to think about was me.

The recovery unit was a 12 step based program and at the end of every day the minibus would take us to various AA meetings in Scarborough, Whitby and Pickering. We were strongly encouraged to attend as many meetings as possible and to engage in the 12 step recovery program. I loved these meetings. For once I was talking to people who spoke my language. The language of an addict.

These new friends and meetings were like my new local, only this time I would get soberer and soberer the longer I stayed.

If you are in recovery you will know exactly what I mean, addicts speak a different language to other people and we can work out a fraud in seconds. All respect to people who work as therapists, but I don't think for one moment you will ever understand an addict, unless you too are recovering from addiction. We will see right through you and you wont really be able to help us. Where necessary we will manipulate you.

If you're reading this and you are still in active addiction, then my friend there is hope. If I can get clean and sober after the life I lived, then you can too. Go to an AA or NA meeting if you're able, or go to the doctor and see if you can get into a rehab or go to a church..

Some churches are affiliated to funded recovery centres and help get you a place. Many of these free places have a wonderful christian ethic. Sober houses to live in and jobs to learn, in various locations around the country. So just because you have no money, there is help. I was a hopeless drunk drug addict and I had to get away from my local area to get well.

Too many people were toxic and would have done their best to foil my recovery.

In fact on my first visit home, an old drinking buddy thought it would be funny to bring bottles of beer when he came to see me. I didn't find if funny, there really was nothing about what I and my family had gone through that was remotely funny.
If you are struggling, there is help. Brothers and sisters, I am saying a prayer for you all now..

'Lord help the reader of this who needs you now to find the courage to make today their last drink or drug'
Amen

The next few weeks were very traumatic, as the therapy sessions and AA meetings continued I began to realise more and more about my life decisions. I was a defective character and I was starting to see just how messed up my life had become. Jane's husband and my wife at the time both became aware of our affair and the world turned upside down again. Emotions were high and I was delivered a letter from my wife's solicitor requesting a divorce. Despite being clean and sober, I was still hurting everyone. It was not supposed to be like this.

And to think, I'd had a going to rehab party, with the idea that I would return all fixed and mentally healed and everyone would cheer as the prodigal son retuned, ready to continue on where I'd left off. It was becoming very clear that this was never going to be the case.

Our Step 4 & 5

Step four and five are the most powerful of the steps. They urge you to look inward at your life and examine everything you've ever done as far as you can remember, and to write it down, warts and all, and then share it out aloud with your AA sponsor.

Unfortunately and very sadly, my wife at the time really didn't know who she was married to, I'm not proud of this and there's things she never needs to know. I have since made amends to her and set her free from my poisonous lies.

However, Jane and I decided to start telling each other about our lives. We stayed up all night revealing to each other, our darkest and depraved secrets. We shared ever thing we could ever remember doing that was shameful and wrong. If we were to move forward with our relationship, it was only fair that we both knew what we were letting ourselves in for. It was a brutally honest night and by the morning it was clear that there were only three people in the world who really knew us.

Me, Jane and God!

And, If Jane still wanted me now, knowing all these things, then nothing could stop us. I told her she was like the missing piece of jigsaw in my life and she agreed she felt exactly the same. We fitted together perfectly and our thoughts were full of amazing plans and promises for the future.

Escape from the nut house

I left rehab a week after Jane, she returned to her home in the west midlands and proceeded to rent a house ready for my release the following week.

This was a sad time for both of our families as they realised we were not going back to them. We both have children and they were stuck right in the middle of all of this. Break ups are never clean and people always get hurt, there was a lot of crying done by all of us. We've done our best over the years to make amends, to varying degrees of success.

Any addiction destroys lives. It impacts everyone involved and the pain lasts for lifetimes. Some families never recover and hatred manifests itself. It is a sad fact that as we recover and go through the cathartic process of a 12 step program, our families get left behind.

It is common to see family members stuck in the past, reliving the tragedy of the event and never moving on with their lives. Resentments fill them and they don't even know it.

We recovering addicts are blessed that we have learned how to deal with all the pent up misery and have our own system to continuously process it. The 12 steps of recovery are an amazing tool that can change lives. There is a sister organisation to AA/NA called Ala-non, which helps non addicted family members process the effects of living with an active addict.

Maybe this is you?

If you or someone you know is living with an addict, please go along to an AA/NA meeting. You will find people who speak 'your language' and understand exactly what its like to cope with us.

In a moment of planned madness, Jane said goodbye to her husband, got in her car, and drove all the way back to the rehab centre in the middle of the night. I couldn't wait to see her again and when she arrived I was so excited. I quietly let her into the facility and after getting my bags we climbed over the balcony outside my room and she whisked me away into the darkness and to our new life. There was no leaving do, no goodbyes, no official paperwork. I just did a bunk, and it was exhilarating.

Our short time living in the west midlands was great fun. We had no responsibilities and Jane and I spent our days going to bingo, eating and going to AA meetings. Recovery was our life and we soon had many friends in the fellowship. I never could have imagined when I was in active addiction, that you could enjoy life without some sort of mood altering substance. But going for meals with fellow addicts in recovery turned out to be a right hoot. Theres nothing quite like the dark humour of a group of people who have stared death right in the eye! And walked away free.

It was during these first few months of sobriety that God started to reveal his plans for us. Remember I said that Jane was my missing piece of jigsaw, well you are about to see just how God has been working in our lives.

Sober holidays

We decided to go on our very first sober holiday, so we booked a week, all inclusive to Lanzarote. In all my years of alcoholism I'd never been on an all inclusive holiday! All that free alcohol and now I didn't want it.

It was whilst we sat on that plane it soon became apparent that our aisle buddy in the third seat along, was a chronic alcoholic. She proceeded to demonstrate to us just what it was like for a normal person to be around an active addict.

She talked rubbish the whole flight, spilled her drinks on us and drooled as she passed out, falling asleep on Janes shoulder. But, despite this horrifying display, what both Jane and I noticed, was that under the seat in front of us, was a single piece of jigsaw. It made me think of our conversation that night in rehab about us being each others missing piece of jigsaw and there right between us was a real missing piece! My mind was tickled by the sight of it and I wish I'd picked it up, but we didn't say anything to each other for a little while. Unbeknownst to me for now, Jane had also noticed the little piece and had thought exactly the same thing. Was this God talking to us?

It was a peculiar holiday. I was bored senseless and It became clear that Jane didn't like to walk anywhere. A walk for me is usually at least 6 miles but preferably about 13. I don't like to potter about looking in shops.

What are you actually supposed to do when you are on holiday? If your not slurping sangria or making the most of happy hour, what is there to do?. We endured the week in the sun, before returning home, only to book another two week holiday in Egypt. We had nothing else to do and it was so exciting.

These were the days of 'teletext' holidays, and you never really knew what unrated dump you were going to end up in. On the Egypt holiday Jane ended up having to teach the kitchen staff how to cook and how keep food hot!.

It was on this holiday in El Sid, Sharm El Sheik, that we nearly got talked into buying a time share. We were completely taken in by the sales patter and with our mental image of spending all our sober time relaxing, we thought we'd take it up. It was only when we came to pay that my precious lifetime shenanigans presented themselves. I was totally unable to get any credit due to my dubious credit history, and dubious prior financial activity. I do believe now that God was helping me by not allowing me any credit, we literally escaped years of extortion by the skin of our teeth.

The madness of an addict was still very much alive in both of us, and ridiculous decisions were never far away.

It was at the 'Egyptian history night buffet and show' that we were seated at a table with three other English lads. The waiters thought they were doing us all a favour, being English and all that, but Jane and I were a bit concerned, as we didn't want to be sat with people who were going to drink alcohol all night. It was when the waiter took our drinks order and one by one we all ordered soft drinks, that we all looked at each other, and the conversation turned to AA.

Not one of us sitting at that table ordered alcohol, it turned out we were all walking the same path of sobriety. What are the chances of that eh?. Any other combination, for us or them, could have turned out very messy! And potentially fatal.

I look back and I see God at work, right at the beginning of my path. Amen

The silver piece of jigsaw

The next couple of months saw us take a trip up to Berwick-upon-Tweed to visit my parents. It was on this first visit that we were in my parents kitchen talking one morning, and we noticed a small jigsaw piece on a chain, hanging on the key rack. It immediately attracted our attention and we enquired about its origin. 'Oh, that', my Dad said, 'I found that this morning while I was out with the dog'. Well, well, well, another jigsaw piece.

It was at this time Jane turned to me and started to ask me if I'd seen the… 'the jigsaw piece on the plane?' I finished. 'Yes, she replied excitedly, the one under the seat in front of us!'.. We both looked straight at each other and felt a strange tingle run down our spines. They say if something occurs twice it is coincidence, but three times is a pattern. This was definitely very, very strange and even my mam commented on the unusual 'frequency' of the appearance of these little pieces of jigsaw.

There must be quite a few puzzle enthusiasts who are cursing the hole in the middle of their puzzle, but for us, the picture was only just starting to show itself!

Whilst in the beautiful north east, I took my lovely Jane to Eyemouth to see the seals and eat some chips and whilst there we popped our heads into the little jewellers shop on the high street, to see how much our wedding rings were worth. Its a lovely little shop, run by a family and as we browsed, we noticed the jewellery jumble tray. It was right there, in the middle of all this jewellery, framed by every odd piece of silver you can imagine was, yep, you got it, a single silver jigsaw piece! It was shining out from the middle of that tray, shouting look, I'm with you.

You know when you get that strange feeling and your spine shudders and every hair on your body stands up, well that was what we felt right then. These reoccurring jigsaw pieces we're really starting to attract out attention. And in my head I thought to myself, 'Im going to buy that for my Jane'. The only really big problem was my finances. I had a bank card, as my wife had given it me back, but even after years of work and having two businesses, I was worth the grand sum total of £9.76. You can't even get that from a cash machine as the smallest notes they dispense are tenners. And there was no such thing as contactless in 2008. So I decided that I would sell my wedding ring when I got chance and hopefully have enough to buy the 'silver' missing piece of jigsaw.

Whilst up in Berwick, Jane couldn't help but notice, that compared to where she lived in the west midlands, house prices were super cheap and the place is a million times nicer. It was at this point that Jane had a phone call and had to return to her former home to sort out some legal stuff.

We both agreed that I would stay in Berwick, see my children for a few days and go view a house that was for sale, that had attracted Jane's attention. I was instructed to take a video of the house and see if there was anything I could do with it and report back her with my thoughts. I may not have had any money, but I had flipped a few houses and worked in the building trade for years. I knew how to make money, just up until now I wasn't very good at keeping it..

As I was staying at my parents house, we had arranged for my two boys to come to join us for a little holiday, and see their me and their grandparents. I took my youngest son, who was just 5 at the time, to come along and have a look at this house with me and we both trotted off into town excitedly.

The house was actually two, three storey victorian townhouses, crudely knocked into one, set off the high street down a pedestrian alley and it took us a while to find. It was in a terrible state of repair, literally falling apart and there wasn't a thing that didn't need doing.

Phone based sat nav was not a thing then, so we went round in circles asking people before eventually finding it.

The estate agent met us there and let us in to explore this dilapidated property. My son went scurrying off in one direction and I went the other.

I got really excited, this place looked just the job. It was in a terrible state of repair, literally falling apart and there wasn't a thing that didn't need doing. However, I could easily imagine it as three flats. All it needed was a few moved walls and a blocked up door here and there. (I write this today, whilst sat in what is the top floor flat, listening to the seagulls as Jane hoovers around me).

BUT…and are you ready for this!!… 'Daddy, Daddy… look what I've found!'. Elliot was shouting excitedly from the other room and as I walked towards him he ran out through the door with his little hand in the air and says…..

'Daddy, look what I found, a little piece of jigsaw!'.

My heart skipped a beat, every hair on my body stood up, supercharged by static and I trembled as I saw Elliot holding a tiny little jigsaw piece in between his little tiny beautiful fingers. God was speaking directly into my life. These jigsaw pieces were popping up all around us, they must mean something..

I excitedly called Jane who was buzzing with the news. The jigsaw piece was clearly meant as a sign, to us, from God and It must certainly mean that we should buy the property. So buy it we did.

We then spent a year or so converting the house into three fantastic one bedroom flats, just as I had envisioned the day God revealed himself to us.

We lived in the building as we renovated, we didn't have the luxury of another house to live in. We camped in the old kitchen on the ground floor, with rats running through the walls at night. Our door was an old curtain and we bathed in a bucket with water heated by a little wall mounted boiler. Jane kept the place clean and everything we both now owned, fitted in that small room. All our visitors loved the little room. You could lean out of bed and pluck items from the fridge! We both knew that wouldn't be forever and compared to an alcoholic drunken existence in a grand house, this was actually heaven.

In the time in-between Jane going back to the west midlands and me viewing the house, I had a small financial credit into my account. I realised that with this and selling my ring, I would have just enough to buy the silver jigsaw piece along with a chain. I just hoped that it was still there!, and as I arrived in Eyemouth making my way to that little shop, my heart lifted when I saw it was still in the tray and very quickly it was polished and in a box ready to present to my lovely lady Jane. I knew she was going to love it.

A few days later I was on a train back to the west midlands, to see my Jane and I was getting so excited to see her face when I gave her the gift.

She loved it, she was my missing piece, just like I'd told her in rehab and Jane has never taken it off since that day. Wherever we go, everyone always comments on it.

It always starts a conversation that leads to Jesus. Many of the people we know take great joy in seeing when the next piece reveals itself and what it means. Even now 16 years on, those little pieces present themselves at crucial points in time.

In Alcoholics Anonymous you are asked to believe in a higher power. Originally, the AA big book spoke of God, but everything is sadly secularised today and you're told to believe in a power greater than yourself.

Giving an addict the option to choose their own higher power quite often leads to some ridiculous outcomes, unfortunately these misguided solutions sometimes end up in death or insanity.

I was in no doubt that God was God. He is the higher power of a 12 step recovery and I had no problem with this idea. After all, when left to my own power, I was unable to stop drinking or drugging. Our own power, no matter how strong we think it is, will never come close to the power of God. With him all things are possible.

Things in life were really starting to look up. I am quite a competent all round handyman and Jane had some money, so putting those gifts together and suddenly that old house in Berwick was looking promising. And great news, our offer hd been accepted on the property. We were going to be moving to Berwick-upon-Tweed. We were so excited to call my parents and tell them the great news. Then we would ask if we could stay with them for while, whilst we renovated.

A stroke of luck

Before I had the chance to dial my mams number to tell her the great news about our impending move, my mobile phone rang. It was my Mam and it was not good news. My Dad, whilst visiting my sister and her partner in Northern Ireland, was in hospital after having a severe stroke. He was not well, and we needed to get on the very next flight to Londonderry, where my sisters partner would collect us and take us straight to the hospital.

Now as my sober life has gone on, it becomes more and more apparent that God is very real. My Dad had a stroke only fifteen minutes from the main hospital in Colraine, which turned out to be very important. But not just that, only the day before, the hospital had taken receipt of a new clot busting drug and my Dad was going to be the first person to try it. My Mam and my sister had to sign waivers against the potentially deadly side effects of the drug, however, knowing my that Dad would rather be dead than paralysed, the doctors administered the injection.

His recovery was truly miraculous. Within just a couple of days, his body had uncurled, his speech was recovering and my Dad was returning to us all. If you met him today 15 years on you would never know he'd ever had a stroke. Though he does come out with some very funny special words, like 'fluffleduster', which is obviously the new word for a 'towel'.

The drug was so successful that the local newspaper interviewed my dad and followed up the story a year later. He really did have a stroke of luck being where he was that day. I would like to think Gods guiding hand was at work in all the people involved, as if any part of that equation didn't line up, I would be telling a different story.

So, at this point, I am clean and sober for the first time in my life, I am moving back to Berwick, just down the road from where my parents live and I am in a position to help them. After all they had done to help only 6 months earlier, it was the least I could do for them. Once again God is working to put us all where we need to be, when we're needed. And the amazing miracle is that I am actually starting to see him at work!

My Dad was now recovering well, and Jane and I had moved to Berwick to start the long job of creating three flats from a dilapidated building. It was hard. We had very little money and what money we did have was spent on petrol travelling to AA meetings every other day, sometimes 100 miles at a time. We went to AA meetings just about every other day, to one meeting or another.

AA kept us sober, gave our lives meaning and we thrived, getting further away from our last drunk and finding happiness in the little things in life.

The 12 steps taught us how to live a happy sober, clean life. We threw ourselves into service, volunteering for positions to help wherever we could. We sponsored other recovering addicts, helping them through the 12 steps. God really was working in our lives and we knew it. Though we didn't get the Jesus connection yet.

My Mam and aunty were amazed at the jigsaw story and loved the serendipity of God's hand at work in such an unusual way. They both revelled at the next 'jigsaw' instalment.

We finished building the flats and decided to put them on the market. We knew we should make a few quid and we could look to do another property up. Only in 2009, the housing market crashed and we couldn't sell them….but, here we go again, God has plans! We were left with no other financial option other than to rent the flats out. I believe that this was God's plan all along, as it provided Jane and I with an income. Life had just got a little easier.

The bells

At this point, Jane had just sold her late fathers house in the west midlands and with the money we decided to buy another doer upper. Once again, I had to view a property on my own, I think Jane was off to the west midlands again for some reason, so I went along to view a house on Church Road in Tweedmouth. My Mam and aunty were around and they came along with me. It was there, right in front of the house as we walked to the door that my Mam, aunty and I stopped and looked down at the pavement. Right there, in front of the door, directly outside the house was a single piece of jigsaw! My Mam shrieked and my aunty nearly passed out; I just stared down at the ground.... Hello again God, I take it this is where you want us be.

Now lets see why…

So renovations began in earnest and soon each day was a routine of sanding, filling, cutting, painting, plumbing, wiring etc.
When I work I don't stop for breaks or lunch, I just keep going until I get clumsy and then I stop.

Some days were longer than others and some days I couldn't work because of my mental health issues. By now I was regularly seeing both a psychiatrist and a psychologist weekly. My head was a mess.

I think I've drank too much and smoked far too much weed and probably taken LSD a few too many times. Anyone who thinks weed is benign and is harmless is a deluded fool.

I can promise you, that after a while weed makes you paranoid and neurotic, I became delusional, suicidal and manically depressed. At one point I was smoking nearly an ounce a day just to feel normal. It got very expensive.

It was in-between work days and dark days that I kept hearing it, and there it was again. Bells ringing, every few days, bells. I soon worked out it was the church at the bottom of the road and on Wednesday and Sunday the bells rang the call to worship. I didn't go to church at that time, so why did I feel like those bells were calling me?

I made a secret decision to go to the church the next time they rang. That was on some random Sunday in 2010, I think. But that's not the point really, the fact is I got up, dressed nicely and made my way on the 100m walk to the church. And thats where I met Matthew.

Matthew was the new vicar at Tweedmouth Parish Church and he welcomed me like a brother he'd not seen for many years, and as I entered the typical C of E Church with its towering roof and traditional church smell, the smell of old people and wood. I felt a familiar over bearing vastness but a strange comfort. tI remembered as a child going to Blyth methodist church with my Mam and it took me back to those days of Sunday school and coffee mornings.

I was mad very welcome and I fondly remember Ade, an old lady who loved Jesus so much. She always spoke kind words and seemed to enjoy talking to me. She would encourage me to seek the lord and get to know Jesus. She gave me a smooth pocket sized olive wood cross to take with me and I still have it to this day. I went to Ade's funeral a few years later and it was sad, but I know for her, life was just beginning in the arms of the Lord. When you meet people who love Jesus, you can see it and feel it around them.

Matthew was a very pro active vicar, with a lovely young family and his wife always helped with Sunday school and other stuff with children. He was determined to bring his church right into the 21st century and started bible groups, coffee mornings, extra sermons etc and It wasn't long before he asked me to join his new Alpha course. If you've never been on one and have no idea who Jesus is, or if there really is a God, then this course is definitely for you. At least at the end you can put your hand on your heart and make an informed decision about where you want to go in life.

The Alpha course was amazing! It asked questions of me that I didn't know existed and answered questions in me that needed to be answered. Amazing things happened over those 10 weeks. I was with a group of people I'd started to get to know very closely. Bonds are formed on these groups that you will never forget and as the weeks went by we all grew very close.

The final 'Holy Spirit' away day saw revelations and tears and Jesus was with us all, as we came to know our Lord and saviour. After this, fuelled with a passion to know more, my wonderful, beautiful and kind friend, Mary started a home group bible study and we all continued on for years, exploring the Bible together and really getting to know Jesus. We ate home cooked biscuits, drank buckets of tea and even went out to play crazy golf from time to time. Living a life filled with the joy of the Lord is amazing, and I highly recommend it to you all.

As the years passed I got confirmed and Jane ventured into the church to see this. The only other time she came to church was for the Christmas carol service. But her time was yet to come and the seeds had been sown.

Matthew started an additional modern evening service and along with a couple of other lads, I was asked to form a band of sorts. I played guitar, Alan on piano and another fellow who's name I cant remember played the drums. The services were uplifting and a little deeper than the usual Sunday sermon, digging deeper into Gods word and singing modern worship songs. Slowly, the drummer left and the Alan went off to the London school of music to study, so the band became me. The evenings developed and Matthew encouraged me to pray and lead service, so my new role of Worship leader was born, and I loved it. It was a popular evening session and Matthew and I got on well. The congregation grew and more and more things went on in the Church.

It was around this time that Jane was starting to get jealous of Jesus. I was full of the holy spirit, bible studies and cake sales and was looking into volunteering at big church events and conventions, but Jane, knowing all about my dark past, wondered what my intentions were. This caused us all sorts of issues and slowly, to keep her happy, I drew away from the church.

When you start to leave a church nothing much happens straight away, but eventually like a coal falling from the fire grate, I was warm for a while and then very slowly began to cool right down, and before I knew it I was no longer thinking about church. Life started to take over, and things and stuff started to take precedence. A life with God is amazing, but we are warned in the bible about where we stand. It is better to not know God than it is to walk away.

Revelation 3:15-16

"I know your deeds, that you are neither cold nor hot. I wish you were either one or the other! So, because you are lukewarm—neither hot nor cold—I am about to spit you out of my mouth".

With these words, Jesus gave both a frightening threat and an appeal.

Despite these threats in Revelations, God had not abandoned me, and, as he has a plan for all of us, lurking in the background, he would watch and guide me, revealing from time to time that he was still there. Like a parent who's child has gone astray, you will never stop loving them, you wait and pray that one day, like a lost sheep, you will return to the fold. In fact Jesus tells us that, even though he has the 99 sheep safe and sound, he will search the wilderness to find the one lost soul. Jesus was sent to gather the 'lost' and the sinners, just like me.

Maybe this is you?

Luke 15:1-7

The Parable of the Lost Sheep

15 Now the tax collectors and sinners were all gathering around to hear Jesus.

2 But the Pharisees and the teachers of the law muttered, "This man welcomes sinners and eats with them."

3 Then Jesus told them this parable:

4 "Suppose one of you has a hundred sheep and loses one of them. Doesn't he leave the ninety-nine in the open country and go after the lost sheep until he finds it?

5 And when he finds it, he joyfully puts it on his shoulders

6 and goes home. Then he calls his friends and neighbours together and says, 'Rejoice with me; I have found my lost sheep.'

7 I tell you that in the same way there will be more rejoicing in heaven over one sinner who repents than over ninety-nine righteous persons who do not need to repent.

…..And the jigsaw pieces kept appearing. But only when Jane and I were at a crossroads in our life, not knowing where to turn, did God reveal our next step. In life we don't really need to know the whole journey, we just need faith that the next step is sound.

Jeremiah 6:16

16 This is what the Lord says:

*"Stand at the crossroads and look;
    ask for the ancient paths,
ask where the good way is, and walk in it,
    and you will find rest for your souls.*

MALTA

On a trip to Malta we stayed in St Pauls Bay. We walked the coastal promenade up to Valetta, to meet an old school friend of mine who was living there. At this time we were selling a house in Tweedmouth, but we had found nowhere to move to, we just couldn't see where to go, but, we were also not worried or concerned, as I'm sure you are getting to know why. Its difficult to 'not worry', anxiety comes easy, but it is not helpful. However we knew God had our backs. (Though Jane didn't yet know Jesus)

Anxiety is a fruit of the devil and is an absence of God. We are encouraged not to worry in the Bible.

Matthew 6:25-34

Do Not Worry

25 *"Therefore I tell you, do not worry about your life, what you will eat or drink; or about your body, what you will wear. Is not life more than food, and the body more than clothes?*

26 *Look at the birds of the air; they do not sow or reap or store away in barns, and yet your heavenly Father feeds them. Are you not much more valuable than they?*

27 *Can any one of you by worrying add a single hour to your life?*

We had absolutely no idea where we were going to move to, because God had not revealed that step to us yet. We knew however, that he would, as always, keep us safe and guide us well. We sat in the sun drinking coffee and eating cakes, reminiscing about old childhood antics and trying to describe to my friend all about these amazing breadcrumbs that our God was laying before us. We tried to do this without him thinking we were completely mad.

The serendipity of a journey with Jesus has always made absolute sense to us, but the devil gets into your head as you try to describe these kind of things to the secular world and its easy to wonder if its all real. Even my sister thinks I just make it all up. I pray for her every day.

I did my best explaining. He raised his eyebrows and we laughed, so we just enjoyed the day for what it was, knowing that seeds had, once again, been sown. After saying cheerio for now, we headed off, navigating the little winding streets of this ancient Maltese capital.

And, as we took a few more steps, there, right in front of us on the cobbled alley floor, glinting its colours in the sunshine, was another little tiny jigsaw piece. Jane and I actually laughed out aloud at the appearance of yet another missing piece. We knew that very soon we would be introduced to God's amazing plan as it unravelled in front of us. And my goodness, was this next plan a big one! Its like driving to a destination with your satnav only showing you the next turn and never where you'll end up.

John 8:12

"When Jesus spoke again to the people, he said, "I am the light of the world. Whoever follows me will never walk in darkness, but will have the light of life.""

It waited 2 years

Jane is a master of patience when it comes to looking on the computer for houses. Her eyes are guided like a laser targeting system, specially formulated to find the next project. And there it was, an ex council office building, a Georgian hall, grand and dilapidated, flaking paint and a clear absence of love and it had just come back on the market after two years. Someone had been trying to get planning consent and after spending thousands and getting nowhere, they had pulled out. It was cheap and it was now available. The minute we viewed it and walked up the un-loved, but potentially beautiful returning staircase and opened the door into the grand hall I said yes.

God really had some grand plans for us. I could see beyond the wallpaper hanging from the ceiling and the boarded up fireplaces. I could see majesty and magnificence.

It soon became ours and as we delved into the history of the building we found out that not only had it been the church hall, but it was once part of the new temperance hall! That used to be at the rear where a car park now stood. The temperance movement believed in absolute abstinence of alcohol, quite fitting for a couple of drunks. Bizzarely my grandma on my mothers side was from a family of Temperance followers. There is no such thing as coincidence.

Over the next thirteen months and ten days I laboured non stop on this massive renovation project. Jane found a job working for lady with a B&B in town.
Inch by inch we built walls, knocked walls down, added bedrooms, bathrooms, en-suites, coving, ceiling roses, the full shebang. The cracks outside were filled and painted, windows rubbed down, primed and re glossed.

And all the while, as I worked, people stopped me to tell tales of playing badminton in our living room, watching cub scout gang shows and having Christmas parties with the church. There was an old brass name plaque on the front wall. If you looked sideways, with the light in the right direction you could just see the original name, Wallace Green Hall. This sounded very grand indeed. The vicar of the church over the road got to hear about this and after a little chat, I offered him the plaque for his church archives. It was an intensive but interesting build, but eventually it was all done.

It was beautiful, we had five foot crystal chandeliers in the main hall hung with 190 separate crystals. Fitting it to the 14 foot ceilings with my dad, was like a sketch from only fools and horses, but we managed, with only a few hilariously worrying moments.

Wallace Green Hall really stood out on the street. The building had never been a home before and the result was dramatic. So, inspired by Jane's tales from the B&B she worked at, I decided we would run a B&B too!

People came from all over the world to stay with us. You see, the thing about recovering addicts, is that when they do something, they do it at 200%. We were quickly rated 9.9 on the internet review sites and joined the heady heights of being one of the top 2 guest houses in Berwick.

We offered grand accommodations and unrivalled candlelit breakfasts, with haggis and freshly baked cakes galore.

The guests loved it, and returned over and over to experience the very best we could offer. During all this time the property was on the market. We had bought it to sell, it was our next stepping stone on our journey. It wasn't time to stop yet.

The B&B brought us a good return to our investment and it was just a matter of time before we had a buyer. It was time to move again. As usual we dint know where yet, but the road travelled with God is full of surprises and adventure, all you have to do is trust him.

Proverbs 3:5-6

"Trust in the Lord with all your heart, and do not lean on your own understanding. In all your ways acknowledge him, and he will make straight your paths."

     Our journey took us from a huge mansion to a tiny one bed cottage and life was great. Hardly any cleaning to do, minute bills and a really quick renovation. Five weeks in total for this one.

     From starting with less than a tenner, life was really taking a turn. Hard work and a positive outlook, with no drink, drugs or take aways kept our bank account healthy. If we couldn't afford to buy it outright, we didn't have it. A lesson I wish I'd learned a long time ago.

     Millions of people in this world are living miserable lives. They don't know it but their every decision is being driven by Satan. We are constantly being made to feel inferior and inadequate unless we have the next new thing: the phone or the car, confounded by constant internet pressure to look a certain way, or dress in certain clothes and that if you don't follow the influencers, then you are obviously a loser!

Unfortunately this drives people into anxiety and massive debt. Bills looming over them every day, just to pay for rubbish that they don't really need. Thirty pounds here, twenty pounds there, a coffee in a branded coffee shop, nails done, lips plumped, gym membership etc. It all adds up. The wages come in on a Friday and by midnight the never never has taken it all away. Back to square one. I know so many people who constantly wish their precious time away, desperately wishing for Friday to come, just to dread the certain recurrence of Monday. All this stress just to keep up with the Jones's.

Time Is the most precious gift we have and to wish even a minute of it away is an avoidable tragedy. But, it is the unfortunate situation that the world is in today and the devil is laughing out aloud at our gullibility.

Maybe this is you?

Jane and I had a conversation about going away in a motorhome. She wasn't sure if she like it and considered renting one. Once we did our sums, it actually worked out that it would be cheaper to buy an old one, go away in it and if we didn't like it, we could sell the motorhome and cover our costs. We had nothing to lose

So we bought an F registered, 1989, 30 year old seven grand motorhome from Barry at Somerset Trade Campers and headed off on an adventure.

We trundled down to Portsmouth at 65 miles per hour, stopping along the way to see friends at various locations and to visit the odd National Trust property. It took us nearly a week to get to the south coast and we were already having a great time. Soon we were boarding a ferry to Santander. It was so exciting, like being children again, going away for the first time.

As a child my parents would take us to the south of France every summer holiday, with a trailer tent in tow. My sister and I were so lucky and relished these journeys to foreign lands. In the 70s and 80s France really was a world away, with different foods and money and you knew you were abroad, everything was different, it even smelled stranger. Along the way we would collect all sorts of French things to bring home.

We would show our friends from school these foreign products and we always had a 'French meal' with our favourite friends on our return. Orangina in its little round glass bottle was so exotic!

Our motorhome adventure took us to obscure and random places in Spain and we headed for the familiar holiday destination of Benidorm for a few days.

It's great, the roads are always clear when your motor homing, this is because everyone is in a traffic queue beyond you. If you set you phone sat nav to avoid tolls, motorways and dual carriageways, your journey takes you on some crazy routes. We went through farmers fields and ended up on narrow mountain passes, with looming drops and the occasional white painted 'safety stone'! Our old Talbot express strained its way up some of the mountain passes and we chuckled as the 60hp engine often never left first gear, screaming its way to altitude.

It was coming down the side of Mt Ventiou in the southern French Alps, that I 'boiled the brakes' on the way down and had no way of stopping! It was terrifying.

This will most likely never happen in a new vehicle and it is quite alarming. However, half an hour of careful engine braking let the fluid cool and soon the emergency was over. Jane fondly remembered her little mini doing the same in 1982.

On a side note. near the summit of Mt Ventiou is a shrine to a Tour de France cyclist 'Tommy Simpson'. He was my Grandfather's cousin and he died whilst racing. He was and still is a 'Tour' legend and I was astonished at how many people from all around the world made their way to the mountain top, to see where he died. It was a heart attack from using cocaine and alcohol during the race. This was the norm back then and I think most racers were at it.

There's a great documentary about him on Youtube. Drug and drink issues have plagued our family on both sides for generations and as I write this…

'I pray that my sons will not fall foul of its misery and that they also come to know the Lord'. Amen

After our preliminary 6 week motorhome adventure, we stayed at Santander in Northern Spain for a couple of days, before we caught the ferry home. If you've never been there, I highly recommend it, Santander is beautiful city, set on a hilly ridge, overlooking the sea, beautiful beaches framed by snowcapped mountains. You can even go skiing within an hours drive of the city.

It was as we stayed here on Easter weekend that we came across the 'Semana Santa' (holy week) Christian parades. They are a sight to behold. Every church, school and musical band are involved, and everyone and I mean, everyone is involved. All the children and adults come out to watch and support the event. The churches parade huge life size effigies of Jesus in various situations across Easter week. From the spectacular Palm Sunday parade, right through to the Biblical account of the resurrection. One can only imagine what it was actually like to have been there when Jesus came through the streets of Jerusalem 2000 years ago. But being part of one of these parades, which occur in nearly every town in Spain, is beyond description. The atmosphere of anticipation is alive, with people jostling for a view. Everyone is letting the old or young move the front, any house lining the street with a balcony, rents the space for viewing guests.

People are dressed in their finery and no-one wants to miss the sight. If there had been a sycamore tree there I'm sure people would have been up it, like Zacchaeus, the little tax man who was desperate to see Jesus.

Luke 19

1. Jesus entered Jericho and was passing through.

2 A man was there by the name of Zacchaeus; he was a chief tax collector and was wealthy.

3 He wanted to see who Jesus was, but because he was short he could not see over the crowd.

4 So he ran ahead and climbed a sycamore-fig tree to see him, since Jesus was coming that way.

      The bands started to play their tunes and the local school children, all dressed in various costumes carry palm leaves ahead of Jesus. And as the life sized model carried by no less 60 men, comes down the street it is clear, that when Jesus came into Jerusalem, everyone in the world at that time wanted to see him. The emotions are electric during these parades and I can honestly say tears flowed down my face.

      We have over the past few years always made our way to various towns in Spain to see these parades, and they are a highlight of our Christian calendar. Easter is by far, more important than Christmas. It is the event that the whole ethos of Christianity is built upon. Without the death and resurrection of Jesus, there is nothing.

Irritating covid

Then, Covid happened. It was the most irritating thing I've ever endured and I don't really want to even write about it. The government was making our lives miserable and stopping us from doing everything. Except for us, we were still able to renovate some houses. Because of Covid, house prices had gone mental and we bought and sold a couple of properties, making more money than we ever expected. We were being blessed in abundance.

We were so fortunate during this otherwise unpleasant time, that we earned enough money from the property sales that both Jane and I were now in a position that we didn't need to work. We retired. Not on a huge amount, but our flat rental income was enough to maintain our low cost lifestyle. When you remove all the rubbish from life, it becomes clear that you need a lot less than you are made to believe. We spent lockdown walking, meeting family and I went paragliding on the sand dunes whenever the wind blew in the right direction. We even managed to head off into Europe in the motorhome, give or take a bit of paperwork.

It was during a lockdown motorhome trip to Morecombe in 2021 that we were presented once more with a jigsaw piece. We knew we were going to be moving, the spider senses were tingling, we just didn't yet know where. We were looking in Penrith,

Workington, St Bees and now we'd seen a bungalow near Lancaster. How were we going to work this one out.

For something to do, we arranged a viewing and it was on the way to that house, that we found the jigsaw piece. After viewing the house it was clear this wasn't the one for us, but we felt guided to look at bungalows. It wasn't long before Jane noticed a probate sale, in the usually expensive, up market town of Morpeth (so they say) and before long we'd booked a viewing. In fact whilst on the phone we were told it had just come up for sale and already a buyer was interested. So we made the offer there and then, and bought it without seeing it. We knew it was right. It was exactly our thing. Uninhabitable and in need of love.

Love we can do. So as the sale went through, we went to see it and instantly saw the potential.

We knew that there must be a reason why we were to move there, after all these years we have learned not to question the big plan. When God asks you to do something, its best to just do it.

It was in Morpeth that some amazing things were about to happen. God was really going for it. Firstly, the bungalow we bought was positioned on a crossroads.

Property over the road was for sale and across diagonally was for sale too. A lady, who had just moved in, popped over to say hi, and was soon drinking coffee and chatting with Jane. She'd come to see what we had done with our house, to get some ideas for hers. It was as she came in that she noticed the crucifix on the wall and she asked Jane if she was a Christian. At this point in time she wasn't and she explained that it was bought from a shop somewhere and it filled a bit of wall.

Jane did, however believe in God, as learned through the 12 steps of AA. But, something happened. This lady watered the seeds that I'd been sowing for nearly ten years.

Matthew 13

23 "But what about the seed that fell on the good ground? That is like the people who hear the teaching and understand it. They grow and produce a good crop, sometimes 100 times more, sometimes 60 times more, and sometimes 30 times more."

Walking in through footsteps of Jesus

On a random Sunday morning in June 2022 the alarm clock shrieked the room awake. 'Come on Derek, get up' said Jane….'were off to Church'!!

My heart missed a beat, I had never heard her say these words, but I was not about to let this moment pass. So up we leapt and after a good few cups of coffee and dressed in our Sunday best, we walked into town to the church the lady across the road had told Jane about. Only today the church was dark and closed? Puzzled we looked around for a notice to say why, I mean, had we got the time wrong, or the venue? A passerby told us that today, the sermon was in the park, outdoors, in full view of everyone. I though Jane was going to pull out through fear. My first venture into church was done secretly, just in case I didn't like it, so I wouldn't have to explain anything to anyone, but no, today it was all in public view.

We made our way to the park and soon we were welcomed by everyone there. The church sponsored an annual fun day, with a BBQ and events etc, but it always began with a sermon and songs led by the worship band.

It was different, but fun, the singing was lively and not your usual old hymns, but rather upbeat modern worship music.

The atmosphere was fun and the park filled with parents and children who whilst queuing up for the free burgers and hotdogs, were doused with the presence of Jesus.

Day 1 of Jane's Christian journey had begun.

We went along to the regular service for the next few weeks and Jane really enjoyed it. Then, it was that time of year again, when we went on our summer motorhome trip. This time we were off for 10 weeks and headed off to France.

By the time we returned in October, brown and a few pounds lighter, we went back to the church in Morpeth. It was a couple of weeks later that a visiting Pastor, an old school preacher, made an alter call at the end of his sermon. He asked us to bow our heads and say the sinners prayer, and that if you'd been moved by it, said it and meant it, then raise your hand. I felt Janes hand go up and with my heart leapt a hundred feet too. Years of patience, years of prayer from so many different people, years of me drifting away, but none the less, here we were, exactly where God wanted us and exactly when. Jane became a Christian and this relit the fire of the Holy Spirit in me. I knew our lives were really going to change.

We both threw ourselves into church life. We volunteered for anything, helped anyone and fed the poor and cold during the winter months. Being retired gave us all the time we needed and its a good job, because we'd never worked so hard for years.

Now that we had Jesus in our lives we decided it was time to get married. We'd live in sin for a long time, but now we were both on the same path, walking a Christian life, we knew it was time to get married, in church in the sight of God!

So thats what we did. It was an amazing day. We married on a Sunday so everyone in our church family could come. We arranged the back hall, with banners and flags, and laid the tables with an eclectic mix of tea sets. People volunteered to help, and so we all muddled together to make the room like a giant vintage English tea party.

Jane walked down the aisle to the song 'Ten thousand reasons' and I cried, tears pouring down my face. This day was perfect, all my family were there, everyone from church attended and the back hall, which had never been set out for 100 people was looking amazing. We said our vows in the sight of God and it was exactly as it should have been. My wife looked beautiful in her silk dress with flowers in her hair and I can honestly say it was one of the best days of my life. Everything was right. When you walk with God anything is possible.

Baptised in the Jordan

Our honeymoon took us to Jerusalem and Tel-aviv. We stayed in a lovely Christian Palestinian family hotel just outside the Damascus gates. We explored every street and stone of that most amazing city, drinking coffee in the only Christian cafe in the Muslim quarter, taking personal guided walking tours and soaking in the history. I remember my old friend Mary from my bible study group in 2015 talking of how she always wanted to go to Jerusalem and walk in the footsteps of Jesus. She'd spoken with such reverence and awe about it, and in such detail ,that I already felt I'd been.

The city is pretty much the same as it was in Jesus's day and you can feel the holy history ouse from it.

We walked to the top of the mount of ascension, praying in the garden of Gethsemane overlooking the old city from across the valley, before visiting the well of Bethesda where Jesus performed miracles. To see where Jesus had to drag his cross was heartbreaking, its hard to imagine unless you actually walk on those cobbled streets to realise the agony he must have been in. It is a very sobering experience. Our walk took us to the garden tomb where Jesus body was laid, and it was just there, on the street outside, as we chatted about our day so far, that we looked at our feet, and all around us, like petals from a shaken rose, were jigsaw

pieces! Hundreds of them! God was all around us and we knew it.
He was also sending us a very loud message and we needed to listen.

What with the move to the crossroads, Jane finding Jesus and our marriage, there was more to come. Much, much more. We took a day trip to Bethlehem and Capernum where Jesus lived and ministered, and then down to the river Jordan. The tour guide, a Jewish historian filled the day with facts and interesting stories. Towards mid afternoon, we went to a baptism site on the river Jordan. It was the place where John the Baptist, baptised Jesus and countless others, some 2000 years ago.

Matthew 3:13-17

The Baptism of Jesus

***13** Then Jesus came from Galilee to the Jordan to be baptised by John. **14** But John tried to deter him, saying, "I need to be baptised by you, and do you come to me?"*

***15** Jesus replied, "Let it be so now; it is proper for us to do this to fulfill all righteousness." Then John consented.*

***16** As soon as Jesus was baptised, he went up out of the water. At that moment heaven was opened, and he saw the Spirit of God descending like a dove and alighting on him.*

***17** And a voice from heaven said, "This is my Son, whom I love; with him I am well pleased."*

The tour guide explained that usually, one or two people would get baptised whilst there and asked if any of us might like this. Well, nearly everyone on the bus raised their hand. He said he'd never seen such a positive response. It also happened that there were two pastors on the tour and they kindly volunteered to baptise us all. I will never forget that afternoon, the sun was shining, the water was clear and the fish were nibbling our toes. We all prayed together dressed in our pure white baptismal gowns, before having a full submersion baptism. An actual white dove flew down as we emerged from the water and you could physically feel the presence of the Holy Spirit. Jesus was without a doubt, right there with us all.

The end of our holiday took us to Tel-aviv for a few days and we walked along the very metropolitan sea front to the old coastal port of Joppa (Jaffa). We visited Simon the Tanners house and discussed the story of Jonah, who set sail from there to try and escape Gods plans. It proves that if God asks you to do something, please, just do it.

Jonah 1

Jonah Flees From the Lord

*The word of the Lord came to **Jonah** son of Amittai: "Go to the great city of Nineveh and preach against it, because its wickedness has come up before me." But **Jonah** ran away from the Lord and headed for Tarshish. He went down to Joppa, where he found a ship bound for that port. After paying the fare, he went aboard and sailed for Tarshish to flee from the Lord.*

(Read the book of Jonah to see how that decision ended!)

Our honeymoon ended after 10 days in the land of Gods wonder and we returned home brimming with Jesus. The holy spirit had blessed our wedding and our baptism and we couldn't wait to share our adventures with our friends.

We will definitely return to that magical country, but the way things are at present, it may be a while.

It was around this time that another Christian couple from church moved to the house over the road and along with their neighbours two doors down, there were now seven of us living on the crossroads. And as you can probably now tell, everything has relevance with God.
You just have to be still, listen quietly and have some faith. God will guide you and he always has a plan.

Jeremiah 6:16

"Stand at the crossroads and look;
ask for the ancient paths,
ask where the good way is, and walk in it,
and you will find rest for your souls.

It was very clear that God was at work in our lives and on our street, but what did he want?.

At the back of our bungalow was an area of garden where nothing would grow and we were racking our brains as to what to do with it. Jane and I were considering getting a crane to hoist a caravan over the fence and use it to help people in need. We'd come across folk through church who could do with getting away for a couple of days. Maybe, we could help. We had the space, the money and the time.

So we prayed for guidance and God gave me dreams.

Job 33:15

He speaks in dreams, in visions of the night, when deep sleep falls on people as they lie in their beds.

Signs and wonders

I had two visions. These were more than mere dreams. Usually, trying to explain any dream to another person leaves you tongue tied. They never make any sense and fade quicker than you can recount them. But in my visions I saw a garden full of people, all with their heads raised and arms in the air, worshipping the Lord, singing and praising and I also saw a fishing net filled with little wooden fish with names on their sides.

I just needed to work out what this meant and what it was we had to do.

I'd booked us an evening with Nicky Gumbal (Alpha course founder) at a church in Newcastle and we were very excited to hear what he had to say. So my wife and I along with the neighbours, headed off for the evening. What we were about to hear was definitely not what we expected.

The theme of the night was the setting up of small group Alpha courses, run from homes or other buildings. The idea being is that some people prefer not to go into a church or church building, but still want to hear what its about. Also, sometimes a course doesn't have enough candidates to run in a large venue, so having just a couple of people in your home can work. In the past Nicky and his wife had done Alpha courses for one person from their kitchen.

There was a lot of food for thought, and that dead garden space was starting to have a calling. It was the next day when the bloke down the road called by, to see if I still wanted to buy his caravan for the garden. We'd discussed it a month back and finally his wife said ok. Unfortunately, when I checked the size, it was too big!

So, we thought to ourselves, God does not want a caravan there, but he does want something!

This was in August and we were heading off to France in the motorhome. We'd recently just purchased a very expensive, new van, and we were all packed for our three month jaunt. Well, so we thought.

We took a ferry to Amsterdam from Newcastle and planned to head through Holland, Belgium and through France and down to Italy, returning up through Austria and Germany. Again, so we thought.

However, God had other plans.

Turn around and 'go home'

Three days into the journey, whilst travelling into France God spoke to me. I know it was him because I heard his voice in 2008 when I nearly died. His voice resounded through my head saying

'Turn around, go home and sell your motorhome',

over and over, so loud I kept looking to see if Jane could hear. It was so distracting that I pulled over to the side of the road. Jane, of course, wanted to know what I was doing, I asked if she could hear it too, to which she replied with confusion. *'What is it you hear?'*

So I told her. I'm not sure what you are thinking right now and I really don't know what you would do, or how your spouse would reply, but, because Jane walks the same path as me, we turned the van around and started to drive back home, as instructed by God..

Our return journey took us through the town of Nantes in North western France. Everywhere we go, wherever we are, no matter what country we're in , we always search for a church to go to on a Sunday and we rarely ever miss the opportunity to worship Jesus.

We found an English speaking church advertised in Nantes and the American outreach pastor, Keith, offered us a place to park our motorhome for the night. We could also join them for worship the following morning. It was a strange affair, which consisted of three houses on an estate. Keith and his wife ran a residential theology school and a house church. This house church idea was new to us, but very intriguing.

Sunday morning came and pastor Keith gave a full on sermon to five of us. Most of the students were away for holidays, but it didn't detract from his thorough sermon and enthusiastic delivery

His word was strong and powerful and he fed our souls. We were then invited to stay on for a fellowship meal and we ended up staying for another full day and night.

We left full of great ideas and a passion for Jesus. If you ever travel via Nantes in France, please stop by and worship with them at Grace Church, you will be made so very welcome.

Eventually, after a few more days, we were back home and parked our motorhome outside our Morpeth house. Immediately our neighbours were intrigued at our very early return, curtains were twitching. None of them were expecting to see us for months, yet here we were back home.

What was wrong?, had something happened? Why were we home so soon?. The kettle went on and we were soon explaining about our message from God and to most of them, our return was the obvious decision.

What with the dreams, the voice of God, the jigsaw pieces in Jerusalem, the home church in Nantes and the meeting with Nicky Gumbal, the area at the back of the house now had a purpose. We had been praying for guidance and it was clear whatever went in that space had to be built to fit.

So, after some 'internetting', we decided we were going to build a log cabin and run home group Alpha courses. So we duly sold our motorhome and ordered a log cabin kit.

Very soon after that a lorry arrived in the street with our flat packed cabin. All the neighbours helped unload it whilst my friend Steven and I built it. That cabin went up in a day, a long day at that, but the ladies kept us fuelled with coffee and cakes, and by the time the sun was setting I'd fitted the final roof shingle. We all sat and ate a delicious fish supper, admiring our days work.

Then it rained non stop for four days and nights. On the fifth day a rainbow appeared over the cabin.

This biblical reference was not lost on any of us and the revelation that the cabin was made from wood from Turkey has an amazing connection.

Noah's ark was set down at the top of Mt Ararat after the floodwaters subsided. The first trees in the new world would have started to grow there, in Turkey about 4350 years ago. The offspring of theses trees were eventually harvested to provide the wood for our cabin. God had already planned our requirements before the first sapling sprouted. It became very clear, once again, that God was very truly masterminding our lives. It was with this that a local pastor blessed and anointed the cabin and all its future works. Amen

We ordered an Alpha course starter pack, a banner for the front fence and then with the love of Jesus in our hearts we headed out onto our housing estate and knocked on doors evangelising and inviting everyone on our first Alpha course.

Knocking on doors can be very intimidating and neither my wife or I had ever done this. But, God gave us all the right words to say. The world is filled with negativity, but if all we did on those outings was to sew seeds, then so be it.

And so Alpha began. Our first course had 8 people attending and as the weeks progressed, bonds were formed and we all got to know each other really well.

We shared weekly meals, watched the videos and had frank and honest discussions.

Alpha and a Demon

On one evening of the course, as we looked at forgiveness, we witnessed the purging of evil spirits from one of our friends. It was a violent evil, that had lived in him for many years and kept him angry. I don't say this lightly, and if you're not a believer you may find it hard to believe. But that anger had lived in our friends head for many years and he constantly relived the traumatic event over and over. When he told us the story, you could see the venom in his eyes, you could hear the strain in his voice as he re-imagined the situation where he got to kill the man who hurt him, his body tensed up, his shoulders squared back and his fists were clenched. He was literally spitting with rage through clenched teeth, his eyes looked black and we all looked on in horror.

This man was completely overtaken by something we couldn't visibly see, but if you could, you would have seen the darkest, foulest creature screeching its way from every part of him. It was like something from a horror film, only this was very, very real. We all prayed for him and as we did, and as he recounted the moment, you could see the strain physically lifted from him, the light returned to his eyes and he almost floated with a peace you could actively see encompassing his whole body.

    The mood in the cabin lifted, like the explosive dawning of the morning sun on a clear day, and everyone let out the breaths we'd all been holding in. Tears trickled down his face and we knew we had just seen a real miracle. The demons that had kept our friend sick and angry for many years were gone! He had been freed from this darkness by the power of the Holy Spirit and we had all been there to witness it. You don't need to believe me and it won't offend me if you don't, but some of you reading this will understand. For those who have never experienced something like this,

'I pray that anyone reading this, maybe one day, you too will experience the amazing power of God in your life. Amen'

12 Steps to redemption

In AA, part of the 12 step program involves a process where you let the darkness out. Bill Wilson and Bob Smith wrote the AA Big book in the 1930's and it was from a God fearing and God understanding Christian based perspective. Like most of life, it has been secularised over the recent years and I believe taking God out and replacing it with a 'Power of your own understanding' is a dangerous option for an addict.

The recovering addicts i've met with the happiest and soundest sobriety, are those who understand that God is God. He is not a wolf, the ghost of granny, the trees of the forest, or anything else, he is God, a power of such magnitude it is impossible to imagine.

Three of the 12 steps are life changing, and if done thoroughly will truly set you free. The demons of our past live inside of us, secrets keeping us sick on a daily basis, the truth hidden from our partners and the terrible 'sickness of resentment'. We re-live the terrible moments over and over again, feeling the same dark emotions as if the act of 20 or 30 years ago had just happened, except each time we feel it again, its power increases and the anger and violence, or misery and shame compounds, like a debt to a loan shark, only this shark has a name and it is Satan.

With resentments, we allow the darkness to live in our heads rent free, these demons take full advantage of this and use the freedom to make our lives miserable and difficult.
Anyone who has done these steps in a recovery program, will know the cathartic freedom the release of our secrets gives.

It is a new life that opens up before you and physically you can feel the darkness being replaced by the light. You can physically feel the freedom as you let every one of the details of your sin filled lives pass your lips in word, to know that someone else understands and that importantly, God has heard you too. These are real demons and expelling them from your life in the most amazing experience. I have often said that it is not just addicts who would benefit from these 2 steps. It is like the sinners prayer, only you actually say it out aloud and share it with a trusted person, exposing every sin you have ever committed!

Maybe you are reading this and fancy freeing your soul this way?

Step 4 & 5 (AA Big book)

4. Made a searching and fearless moral inventory of ourselves.
5. Admitted to God, to ourselves and to another human being the exact nature of our wrongs.

At the end of the Alpha course Jane and I started a series of weekly bible studies, as our group now had a real hunger to understand the word of God. We had an amazing time over that Autumn and winter, looking deeper into the Bible and enjoying the fellowship. We all got to know each other really well and to this day we are all in touch. The cabin smelled deeply of pine and wood smoke from our little log burning stove and the wooden walls were impermeated with prayer and the word of God.

You could feel the presence of the Holy Spirit every time you walked in. Calmness, love and security overwhelmed the troubled soul on entry and banished the worldly scourge of evil. It was a safe space for everyone to share their deepest problems and hand them all over to our loving and eternal Lord. It reminds me of a wonderful promise of calm delivered by Jesus to his disciples, comforting their doubts, and these words are as effective now as they were then.

John 14:1-4

Jesus Comforts His Disciples

1 "Do not let your hearts be troubled. You believe in God; believe also in me.

2 My Father's house has many rooms; if that were not so, would I have told you that I am going there to prepare a place for you?

3 And if I go and prepare a place for you, I will come back and take you to be with me that you also may be where I am.

4 You know the way to the place where I am going."

Do you know where you are going?

Promises made by our Lord are never broken and I live my life knowing that what comes next is the real beginning. If you are doubting or just don't know about any of this, I exhort you to find out what God has planned for you.

We had a lovely blue fishing net hung on our cabin wall and on it are little wooden fish, each with a name and date for the people who found Jesus with us in there.
The visions I had received months earlier were now clear, we built it and the people came, we had become, as Jesus had commissioned us, 'Fishers of People'.

Matthew 4:19

"Come, follow me," Jesus said, "and I will send you out to fish for people."

I feel sorry for the non believers, who think that this amazing world was created from nothing and that every amazing thing you see came about by accident. Science will have them believe that the 'big bang' made everything we see. In my experience, explosions only ever created mess and disorder, I've never seen beauty and especially not complex life come from an explosion. Scientist have never to this day managed to 'create' even a single cell organism, let alone a beautiful creature. Their belief requires far more faith than Christianity and the works of an amazing creator.

So, consider what you believe because the following is worth pondering. You owe it to yourself to actually find out what Christianity is all about, before dismissing the most documented and important event in history. It makes a lot more sense than the man made 'theories' that are floating around.

There are two facts in life that are equally terrifying.

*The first is that '**God is not real**', in which case your whole life, everyone you love, your parents, wife, children, their love for you, the happy times you have together, their beautiful smiles, everything you do, create or experience, all of it, everything your life is, means absolutely nothing, it is totally pointless!*

OR

*'**God is real**', in which case, you need to know what he wants from you and what amazing things he has in store for your life!*

John the Baptist

God has us on the move again. By the easter of 2024, we were ready to head off in our new to us, 22 year old motorhome. The model of this old van is called the 'Pescara', which is Latin for 'abundance of fish' and the reference not lost on us!. And we knew it was for us.

By this time I had also started helping out on the 'Worship on the Street' movement, taking the word of God through song, to the people on the streets of towns all over Northumberland.

If you are a musician, if you can sing, if you love to evangelise or just to stand and pray, then look it up online and join in wherever you are. A love for Jesus is all you need.

So this time we packed the guitar and as we travelled through Spain and Portugal we played and sang on motorhome sites whenever we could, spreading the good news, telling anyone who would listen, about the life, death and resurrection of the most amazing event the world has ever known. The life and works of Jesus are the most documented event in history, ever.

It was in The International Church of the Algarve, an amazing place set up by a traveller thirty odd years ago and which is now a thriving theology college and ministry set in the beautiful 'Vale Judea' (valley of the Jews), near the small town of Loule, overlooking Villamoura and the beaches of the Algarve. It was here that one of the church elders suggested going out on the seafront at Quarteira with musicians and evangelists.

He played a video of the WoTs team in Edinburgh, singing outside the Parliament building on the Royal mile. It is amazing how good news travels fast and far, inspiring Christians across the world.

Around 50 or so people from the church went down to the promenade over 3 evenings in April 2024, with guitarists and singers, people were dressed in 'can I pray for you t-shirts, there were interpreters in many tongues, Ukrainian, French, German, Dutch, Spanish, in fact we were blessed with a truly multi lingual group and with along with the song and prayer, we saw people come to know the Lord on the streets that very night.

I always believe we should not be secret Christians, we need to spread the 'good news', we should sow the seeds everywhere we go and pray that if not now, but later, someone else will water them. The Lord moves in mysterious ways and you never know if you are the one who does the sowing or the watering.

Our time away was a welcome break after a very busy winter season, but it was on our return home that we came across another jigsaw piece and we knew it was that time again. Our ministry is most definitely a mobile one.

We marketed our house and prayed on the direction we were headed, asking for guidance and inspiration. We have never been let down yet and so we started our search for the next place God wanted us. It was a frustrating search and as we put in offers, on houses in and around Morpeth, and these were cash offers, on house after house, the devil reared his head and greed showed itself in every transaction we attempted. Gazumping, a nasty practice banished from house selling in the 1980's is becoming a thing again. We couldn't understand why our offers were not being accepted, and we prayed, 'Lord, where do you want us?'.

Our house soon came under offer, but we still had nowhere to go. The next step was just not revealing itself. So we just handed it all over to God and decided not to worry as whatever was going to happen, would happen.

Then to add complications to everything, one of our long term tenants gave us 4 weeks notice. This was just what we didn't need right now.

The flat was a mess and on top of selling our house, we now had to travel 100miles up and down to Berwick each day to redecorate it.

The flat needed a full renovation, there was nothing that didn't need doing and now we also had the added pressure of having to find a new tenant. It was stress we didn't need.

If there is stress, anxiety and worry involved, then God is not there. It is only the devil that wants you to feel that way.

And then it hit us, we had just not seen it. Where was our faith? God had had already found the new tenants....US. Our journey had started in Berwick and now for a reason only known to God, we were being called back. And, this was so exciting. It is always exciting when God reveals his plans into your life, and it never gets tiring. So we dutifully put our stuff into storage, hired a van and leaving the house empty, made our way to the brand newly decorated and renovated flat. It's the top flat of three, set in the middle of town and the widows overlook the rooftops, with Bamburgh castle and the Holy island of Lindisfarne in the distance. Its our favourite flat and its right next door to the Baptist church. Jane knows the pastor as she used to work with him years ago, and over the years had repeatedly invited us both to his church. Those were the days before Jane knew Jesus.

But, as with everything, there is always a right time and this was it. I hope you can see how God is orchestrating everything we do.

The incredibly friendly people at the church welcomed us with open arms, it really did feel right and we felt at home. Maybe this is why God moved us to Berwick and maybe this is where we are needed.

Over the past few months we have come to meet other people who have felt called to Berwick and I don't think any of it is a coincidence. There is a reason and its going to be amazing. I re-met my old friends from the Tweedmouth church and fires are alight with the love of Jesus. Plans are afoot and the church had been discussing Alpha courses and recovery ministry. They were also intrigued by the worship on the streets movement.

A little cottage came up for sale in the local village of Paxton, situated just a mile into Scotland and our offer was quickly accepted. So, thats where were going, that's where God wants us.

It's quiet and peaceful and theres a lovely walk along the river into Berwick.

There's an old garage on the property which looks perfect for us to create a small accommodation. We are going to use this for anyone who feels the need to get away for a few days or fancies a break.

God always provides. God is good. Our plans from here are being taken a step at time, not only is the Morpeth house sold, but so have our flats, we feel that a season has come to an end and the one next is about to start.

Where life takes from here will be exactly where its meant to go. God guides us every day, and we relish the adventure, there is never a dull moment.

Revelations

The revelation that God has a name, changed my life!

The revelation that a foul sinner like me, a sinner who dished out misery and heartache to everyone I met, could be saved by a man who died brutally on a cross 2000 years ago, so that I could be free. He opened my heart and my eyes to the beauty of the world and to a love available to even me.

If Jesus can save me, then honestly, anyone can be saved. The worse you are, the more Jesus loves saving you.

Remember, at the beginning I told you that

 "All who call on the name of the Lord can be saved".

When God spoke to me saying 'Not like this", as I lay on the brink of death in that old caravan, my heart cried out 'help me'. I called out to a God I had turned my back on, and he answered, and he saved me.

My life was surrounded by darkness, but Jesus has brought the light into my life.

John 8:12 - Jesus said…

"I am the light of the world. Whoever follows me will never walk in darkness, but will have the light of life."

Maybe you feel your life is filled with sin and shame?

Maybe you are lost and feel life is hopeless?

Maybe you want to be free from the demons in your head?

Maybe you suffer from addiction, depression or anxiety?

Maybe you just want to feel loved?

Brothers and sisters….. IF THIS IS YOU….

…then today can be the first day of your new life, a life guided by Jesus.

All you have to do is

'*call on the name of the Lord.*'

'Reader,' I would like to pray with you now

*'Lord you are a God of amazing grace.
You light up the darkness, with a thousand stars.
Everyday you move among us, touching our hearts and inviting us all to know you.*

Lord you saved me from the brink of death and Jesus I ask you to reveal yourself to everyone who reads these words.

Lord Jesus, I know that I am a sinner, and I ask for Your forgiveness. I believe You died for my sins and rose from the dead. I turn from my sins and invite You to come into my heart and life. I want to trust and follow You as my Lord and Saviour. AMEN'

Romans 10:9

*You say to us lord, that,
If we declare with our mouth,
that JESUS IS LORD,
and believe in your heart that God raised him from the dead,
YOU WILL BE SAVED! AMEN*

This can be you!

Jesus loves us all, no matter how dark our paths and no matter what we've done.

The end….?

Printed in Great Britain
by Amazon